The Art of *Weaving* a Life

Other Schiffer Books on Related Subjects

Linen: From Flax Seed to Woven Cloth, Linda Heinrich,
ISBN 978-0-7643-3466-5

And Still We Rise: Race, Culture and Visual Conversations, Carolyn L. Mazloomi,
ISBN 978-0-7643-4928-7

Hmong Story Cloths: Preserving Historical & Cultural Treasures,
Linda A. Gerdner, PhD, RN, FAAN, ISBN 978-0-7643-4859-4

Cover design by Danielle D. Farmer
Keyform weaving instructions and accompanying photos created by Janet Lewis Estell and Richard Merrill
Illustrations and original edition's design by Richard Merrill
Type set in Trajan/Bruce OldStyle BT

ISBN: 978-0-7643-5264-5
Printed in China

Published by Schiffer Publishing, Ltd.
4880 Lower Valley Road
Atglen, PA 19310
Phone: (610) 593-1777; Fax: (610) 593-2002
E-mail: Info@schifferbooks.com
Web: www.schifferbooks.com

For our complete selection of fine books on this and related subjects, please visit our website at www.schifferbooks.com. You may also write for a free catalog.

Schiffer Publishing's titles are available at special discounts for bulk purchases for sales promotions or premiums. Special editions, including personalized covers, corporate imprints, and excerpts, can be created in large quantities for special needs. For more information, contact the publisher.

We are always looking for people to write books on new and related subjects. If you have an idea for a book, please contact us at proposals@schifferbooks.com.

The Art of  Weaving a Life

A FRAMEWORK TO EXPAND
AND STRENGTHEN YOUR PERSONAL VISION

SUSAN BARRETT MERRILL

Instructions by Janet Lewis Estell & Richard Merrill

Schiffer Publishing Ltd

4880 Lower Valley Road · Atglen, PA 19310

ACKNOWLEDGMENTS

This book is the result of many loving hands and hearts. First, my husband Richard, whose patience and support gave me confidence to move forward with this work. He was the front-line editor, and worked tirelessly with me to produce this book.

Grateful acknowledgment is made for the cooperation of the Joseph Campbell Foundation, www.jcf.org, who graciously gave permission to use quotations from Campbell's works. Warmest thanks to Arlene Morris, Dr. Steven Stern, Judy Wick, and to kilim expert Dario Valcarenghi of Milan, Italy.

To my friend, cohort, and contributing author Jani Estell, who accomplished a mighty task in creating the instructions for weaving the keyforms and taking their accompanying photographs. Thanks to her son, Eben, for his hand-modeling, to Jani's daughters Leah and Emily, and to her husband Grant, who assembled the first nine-foot high EarthLoom at the 2005 Common Ground Country Fair in Unity, Maine.

Many thanks to the Wednesday Spinners, who people the pages of this book: my friends, fiber companions, and steadfast adventurers with whom I spin every Wednesday: Claire Agoliati, Nancy Alexander, Roni Bloom, Sue Bushman, Nuna Cass, Sara Christy, Martie Crone, Rae Dumont, Barbara Eggert, Biddy Esher, Jani Estell, Wendy Gignoux, Gail Grandgent, Joli Greene, Louisa Grosjean, Susanne Grosjean, Julie Havener, Kate Henry, Sue Hill, Shari John, Donna Kausen, Linda Kimmelman, Hanne Lewis, Maude March, Penelope Olson, Willow Runningwater, Mary Ann Solet, Lin Sullivan, Cynthia Thayer, Geri Valentine, Karen VanTine, Judy Wick, Chris Yentes, and Charlotte Young.

In memoriam: Mollie Birdsall, Kathleen Bowman, Gail Disney, Jill Evans, and Mascha Litten, we miss you!

Special thanks to Cynthia Thayer, who gave me valuable advice, and to Susanne Grosjean, "Ms. Madder," author of "The Color Red."

My family has given me unstinting love and encouragement: thanks to Beam, Abram, Trevor, Sorcha, Eleanor, Ted, Barbara, David, Carol, Otis, Amos, Lisa, Frank, Peter, Matthew, Ian, Lincoln, Melissa, Julia, and Mackenzie Rose. Many friends helped along the way: Susan and Steve Grabara, Judy Lambert, Barbara and Jeff Merritt, Carmine Leo, Susan Mills, Rob Shetterly, Gail Page, and Daniela Kuper.

Thanks to Bill Mor of Barakat, Inc., for the opportunity to photograph tribal rugs, to the Women's Business Group and Jeff Ackerman of WHCA in Ellsworth, Maine, and to the gang at the Kushi Institute, Becket, Massachusetts.

Thanks to my granddaughter Azria, whose beautiful four-year-old hands are weaving on page 29. And most of all, thanks to my personal trainers, Huzur Maharaj Charan Singh Ji and Gurinder Singh Dhillon of Beas, India.

In addition to her family, Grant, Leah, Emily, and Eben, and the Wednesday spinners, Jani is indebted to her "other" spinning support group, The Black Sheep Spinners (a.k.a. The BaaBaas), and to Kate Nadeau for her friendship, advice, and encouragement.

Wednesday Spinners of Hancock and Washington County, Maine

To the Creator in You

*Zati is an ancient Urdu word meaning "essential,
intrinsic, natural, fundamental."*[1]

*"A Zati or inherent name is an attempted imitation
of the transcendent Sound."*[2]

Zati: a word from the Urdu language (northern India and Pakistan) meaning *essential, intrinsic, natural,
fundamental*; also translated as *from the inside out,* or *from a sacred place.*

The weavings you do can be described with the word *zati,*
because they arrive and are created from the inside out, bringing into being
forgotten aspects of yourself.

CONTENTS

INTRODUCTION

*"The value of a diamond pertains to that diamond
and not to the case in which it is enclosed. We should try to get the
diamond and not worry about its case."*[3]

This book is the case. It is not the diamond, but it may point to the diamond for you. Our weavings are the case: they are manifestations of the formless, in a form. The seven keyforms in this book all point to the diamond within each one of us.

I have lived my life with three questions as steady companions: "Who am I?" "What am I doing here?" and "How can we learn to love each other?" Somehow I knew there had to be a meaning to my experiences. To my mother, a genuine healer, who showed me that the world is more than it appears to be, and my father, a counselor, who held sacred the deep questions, I owe a debt of gratitude which I can never repay. They gave me the gift of their wisdom and encouraged me to find answers through my own experience. So began my decades-long journey exploring the heart of the world. I lived all over the United States and in several countries including Greece, England, and Denmark, and finally traveled many times to India. I became a teacher, a social worker, and a weaver. In this journey, I have realized that a diamond is polished by the grit of experience. Weaving has been a steadfast teacher through all these years.

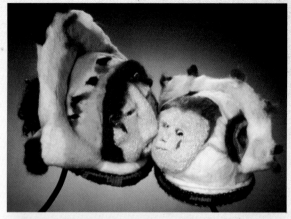

I discovered that weaving is the art of making choices, and integrating those choices into a whole fabric. The activity itself, its quiet gentle pace, brings a feeling of peace. Where does this feeling come from? Could it be that the creation of an integrated fabric reflects a profound inner activity? I began to understand that the phenomenal world of my experience represented a pale shadow of a more subtle truth.

As I worked for peace in the world, I realized that the saying "peace begins at home" didn't mean my home state or my home town, but my own heart. Since then I have been exploring the inner landscape through meditation, and expressing this work through weaving.

The seven keyforms represent seven stages of development of awareness of our inner lanscape. The peace that comes inside when our inner and outer lives are not at war with each other, but are instead woven together, spills over into our families and communities.

In turn, we learn to embrace each other and our world neighbors with the intention of peace by realizing that each of us is a single thread in the whole world fabric.

CHAPTER 1

WEAVING A LIFE

"Our Hands imbibe like roots
So I place them on what is
beautiful in this world.
And I fold them in prayer,
and they draw from
the heavens light."

— St. Francis of Assisi

The Art of Weaving a Life is both a metaphor and a means for building the fabric of the self.

This book is for everyone, even those who have never woven before. Beginning weavers will find basic tapestry techniques; experienced weavers will discover new dimensions in their work, but it is through creative play that our inner values are revealed. Every thread of this web is, by conscious choice, one that delights you. In this weaving journey you are the creator. Your loom is first a mirror to reflect who you are now, then a window to imagine who you would like to become, and finally a doorway through which you will step into the realization of that vision.

Weaving, the interlacing of separate threads into a whole fabric, is a unifying experience. The physical act of weaving itself calms and unifies the body's systems, unlocks energy, relieves stress, and brings you into the present moment.

Weaving is about balance, as you will discover in the thread crossings, vertical and horizontal, one by one integrating every part into a balanced whole.

For over twenty thousand years,[1] people of this earth have been exploring the riches inherent in weaving on a simple loom and the possibilities for the expression of an unspoken language of symbols.

With only a collection of sticks arranged into a stabilized rectangle, generations of women wove, talked and sang their personal and tribal mythologies into weavings they envisioned through the window of their looms. Under the guidance of mothers and grandmothers, girls were initiated into the color red, motifs of the heart and patterns of being human. All these became coded into the fabric of their lives. Thus, weaving a life is not a new idea. The intricate interlacing of threads to depict inner mythic and mystic structures is somewhere a part of our story, and a memory deep within each of us.

Tribal weavings were like scrolls speaking an ancient language of symbols that revealed the relationship between the cycles of life and the greater Self. The "tree of life" pattern, which traditionally expresses mediation between this world and a higher or inner one is a marvelous example. That ancient process of connecting the inner and outer worlds is the work of weaving a life.

The seven-stick loom, which my husband Richard and I developed, is designed to take you on this journey. The Journey Loom is a small version, a handmade tapestry loom as portable as knitting and made for travel; however, any sturdy picture frame or a hard cover book can be used as a loom. You can weave while sitting on the couch, in the woods, at the beach, in the car, in bed, with children or elders. A loom can be as large or as small as you want to make it.

It is the weaving patterns that call you to follow the thread within and explore the hidden form, by weaving two-dimensional flat structures and watching them change into three-dimensional sculptural forms. Each one invites you to tell your own story the way only you can tell it, to allow yourself the play of creation with textured fibers running through your fingers and over the palms of your hands.

The art of weaving a life is the journey to the source of your choices which determine the nature of your experience. It is the apprenticeship to living a conscious and intentional life, and can be part of the preparation to living a spiritual life. It is the process of recognizing, receiving, and living in harmony with our own deepest truths. Weaving a Life embodies a language of transformation. I have called the seven patterns in this book *keyforms,* because each one is both universal form and ancient symbol. Each represents a choice, a stage in the journey of life, or a rite of passage. These seven key-forms map out a fundamental process we all follow at any level, with every choice we make, whose structure is rooted in the natural relationship of awareness and action and in our deepest patterns of behavior. They could be called fractal, because they are true at any scale. The stages of the journey, the terms of this language of transformation, can be applied to one's whole life, to a chapter in it, or to its smallest moments.

The Keyforms are:

1. *The Amulet:*
invoking your beliefs
about yourself.

2. *The Bowl:*
receiving awareness that the
contents shape the vessel.

3. *The Doll:*
recognizing the wisdom
that exists within you.

4. *The Belt of Power:*
delineating yourself as
sacred space.

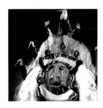

5. *The Mask:*
seeing through the eyes
of the Creator in you.

6. *The Bundle:*
integrating your choice into
your life in action; gathering
the tools of your journey.

7. *The Shawl:*
practicing awareness;
transforming your
beliefs about yourself.

We come of age many times in a life as each rite of passage occurs. In a whole life,

- the amulet could be seen as the keyform of conception
- the receiving bowl is birth
- the doll is childhood
- the belt of power is adolescence
- the mask is adulthood
- the bundle is the mature life
- the shawl is the garment worn in meditation in the journey into the inner life;
  it is also the cloth in which one is wrapped at death.

In another view, these are seven stages on the journey we take to live a spiritual life.

- The amulet is an invocation to awaken to the need for change.
- The bowl is an invitation to see a new dimension of yourself in your desire to find what has lasting value in life, to recognize that you have an inside and an outside, with free flow between them.
- The doll brings you insight into whom you want to become.
- The belt is the choice to make the vision real by delineating a part of your life for it.
- The mask is initiation into the mystery you seek.
- The bundle is the taking on of the responsibility to yourself to fulfill your quest.
- The shawl, traditionally used in meditation, wraps the ego at its death, when the personality loses its power to block the natural spiritual impulse; it represents the practice of stillness in order to go behind the mask of the world.

> "Nevertheless—and here is a great key to the understanding of myth and symbol" says Joseph Campbell, "the two worlds are actually one. The realm of the gods is a forgotten dimension of the world we know. And the exploration of that dimension, either willingly or unwillingly, is the whole sense of the deed of the hero." He goes on to ask, "…how to represent on a two-dimensional surface a three-dimensional form, or in a three-dimensional image a multi-dimensional meaning?"[2]

While weaving the horizontal pattern thread on the loom, we touch each vertical thread of our belief. In just this way, a conscious life is woven thread by thread.

CHAPTER 2

THE STORY OF
THE GRANDMOTHER TREE

We are woven together by invisible threads,
Energetic fields of blooming possibilities.
As a creator, what do you envision?
Can you see the cosmic cloth?
It is your weaving, your dance.
Weaving on the warp of your life,
What is the fabric of your story?

The story of The Grandmother Tree begins with a woman who loved her husband dearly, and took care of him through a long illness. During this time, she also supported the family.

They had a beautiful son, and his mother completely adored him. At long last, her husband did die, and she brought up her son and they had many wonderful times together. He grew up intelligent and handsome. When he became a man, the call came and just as she feared, he did go to war and he was killed. His mother felt bereft, useless and angry. She felt a rage that she thought would never end. She felt as though she did not want to go on any longer, because life had played her this bitter trick.

She took a walk one day far into the woods. As she walked, she realized she had lost the path. She found she did not care. She looked around her, wandered to a sunny spot, lay down in the old leaves and fell asleep. Before long, she heard someone singing:

Hawthorn, hawthorn
Help me in my task
A handful of berries
Is all that I do ask...

She sat up and looked around. Who is that? she thought. Then she saw an old woman by the stream who was gathering hawthorn berries from a tree that was growing there. She walked over to her and said, "What are you doing?"

The old woman said, "I am gathering hawthorn berries. What are you doing in this forest?"

The widow said, "I am lost. I have lost the path."

To which the old woman replied, "Ah, I see, you have lost more than the path."

And with that the widow began to cry and told her whole story. She poured out her heart, telling her about her husband and the illness and her son, her beloved son, how useless life seemed. Then she asked, "Can you help me?"

The old woman said, "Yes. I can help you. But there are three things you must do. First, you must find the pool of Everclear Water and bathe in it until you feel completely washed. Then you must find the Golden Mountain and climb the mountain to the very top. Lastly, you must find the Grandmother Tree, an ancient oak standing at the very top of the Golden Mountain. In her branches is a loom, a rectangle that looks like a door. On this loom, you must weave a gift for the one you love."

With that, the old woman was gone.

Oh, thought the widow, I have no idea where to find these things.

She looked at the stream and thought, "I wonder if the pool of Everclear Water could be at the very beginning of this stream?"

And it was.

A clear, singing, bubbling spring, the most beautiful pool she had ever seen sprang out of the ground from the source of the stream. Pink yarrow flowers grew all around it, soft moss and wild blue iris.

She looked down into the water, it was so clear. She could see smooth colored pebbles on the bottom. It was quite deep. Oh, it was so deliciously beautiful. She took off all her clothes and leapt in. Ah, she thought, this is warm and comforting. She swam and did somersaults and sat on the bottom of the pool and held her breath as she looked at sunlight coming in through the water. Oh, she felt so good in this water. She floated on the top and it seemed as if all her heaviness were washing out and dropping to the bottom of the pool like sand.

After several hours in that refreshing water, she climbed onto the bank feeling very different, very light. She dressed and lay down by the side of the pool where she fell into a deep sleep. She dreamed there were golden leaves falling over her, and that before her was a beautiful mountain filled with autumn sugar maples that sent their leaves like wings to heal her, and when she woke, it was true. There were golden leaves falling all around her and there was the mountain that was covered with golden forests and she thought,

"This must be the Golden Mountain."

And it was.

Very slowly she looked around for a path until a certain opening in the trees seemed to invite her in. Reindeer lichen and winterberry were growing along the rocky path, and deer orchids glowed in marshy places. Spruce and pine were interlaced with the maple trees. The wild grapevines that grew on the granite faces called to her and said "pick me" and she thought, maybe I can use these for my weaving at the top of the mountain. She had to climb over rough stones, but they seemed to help her, almost as though they were showing her the way. And then she saw the little blue forget-me-nots someone had planted long ago. Her heart stopped for a moment but they seemed to be singing to her, "we will help you." In this way she began to pick her bouquet.

9

As she went on she found daisies and clover and Indian paintbrush, which she hadn't seen since she was a child. The whole mountain seemed to be lifting her and showing itself to her. A spruce called her over and offered her some of its long strong thread-like roots. Pointing her fingers straight into the earth, she gathered them with the warm smell of the black soil still clinging to the rootlets as she coiled them like rope. Other plants called to her and seemed to say, "choose us, we want to help you."

She felt loved. She felt the support and embrace of all life around her. She was surprised that there was such a generous loving kindness all the way up the mountain. Finally when she was at the top, she could scarcely believe what she saw. There was a giant oak, spreading her great canopy of branches like sheltering arms. This was the Grandmother Tree; behind it was a cave, a cave that was black inside, filled with complete darkness. On the lowest branch of the tree hung an ancient rectangle made of seven strong sticks. It looked as though this loom had been here forever, reaching from that branch all the way to the ground. It was then that her attention was pulled back to the cave. She felt drawn toward it compulsively, despite her fear of the blackness within.

As she stepped through the loom toward the cave, she realized, "I do not need to go toward that blackness." She turned around. There before her was the most magnificent view. Three mountains with the sun glinting off their peaks, green and red foliage and wide fields. It was breathtaking. This was the most magnificent view she had ever seen in her life. And she realized at that moment that she had a choice. She could look into the blackness of the cave or turn around and open herself to the light.

Oh, she thought, "this is my choice." She sat looking through the loom to the sunlight as she began to string, or warp, the loom with her vines. As she wove, she sang a song:

O Loom
O Loom
Will you help me please?
I want to live a life of peace.

This is what I want. And as she thought it, she had it! She had the loom and the view and a song and she had peace. She wove a most beautiful cloth with the roots and vines and flowers and sewed up the sides with a root to make a container. After she finished her weaving, her heart opened to her life for the first time in many years and she laughed and wept with the gift of the weaving in her hands.

Stepping forward through the loom, she walked down the Golden Mountain past the beautiful flowers, touching them and feeling the end of the day's sun on her back. When she reached the bottom of the mountain, there was the old woman who was gathering the herb heal-all into her apron. As she approached, the old woman said, "Well, now how may I help you?"

And the widow said, "You have shown me how to help myself: I have found my path." And she gave her the weaving as a carrier for her herbs. Thanking the old woman, she felt a light in her heart, and easily found her path home.

CHAPTER 3

THE LOOM: VIEWPOINT

"The work of weaving is a work of creation, a birth.
When the textile is finished, the weaver cuts the threads that link it to
the loom and, while doing this, pronounces a formula,
a blessing that is the same as the one used by the midwife
when she severs the umbilical cord of a newborn child.
Everything takes place as if weaving were the translation of a
mysterious human anatomy into a simple language."[1]

In all the history we know, the nomadic weaver has set up her portable loom and continued weaving. The stories written in wool on the oldest textile fragments found frozen high in the Altai Mountains 2,500 years ago indicate the ability, strength, and vision the weaver sees in her loom. Looms of sticks, and fabrics woven with animal and plant fibers, have long since dissolved back into the earth but their presence in sculpture, paintings, tomb and cave walls is testimony to the antiquity of weaving, and its importance in human cultures.[2]

A loom is a structure on which to weave a web of vertical and horizontal threads. With few exceptions, looms over time have been constructed of wood. Large frame looms are either horizontal or vertical. Four pegs pounded into the earth at the corners of a rectangle, with logs placed above and below each pair, create a "ground loom," a horizontal loom on which many of the world's most complex and exotic rugs have been woven. The Navaho loom is a vertical frame loom with two vertical logs planted in the earth and the frame built on those two parallel poles. Small frame looms can be both horizontal and vertical depending on how one wants to work because they are light and portable. Over time the concept of a loom became more sophisticated; First, a wooden machine with harnesses (holding pattern threads) and foot pedals to open the weaving and change the shed. With the Industrial Revolution, it became a power-driven metal machine.

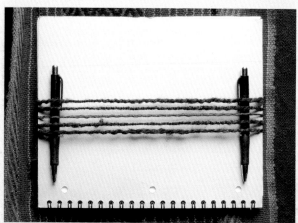

For our purposes, the seven-stick Weaving a Life Journey Loom is perfect. It is light. It fits into a bag the size of a quiver and can be worn like a back pack and carried the world over. When you are ready to weave, take out your sticks and fasten them together in a few minutes and you are weaving. It gives weaving the same immediacy as knitting, a project you can pick up at any time.

When you are ready to stop weaving, the loom easily comes apart with the weaving still on it. Roll it up and put it back in your pack until you are ready to weave again.

But it is also possible to weave on this book! You can use the cover of your notebook or an old picture frame; or you can build your own frame loom.

I like to go to the beach and find seven sticks worn smooth by the tide: Maybe beaver sticks washed out of the lodge, clean toothmarks still visible, or simply salted driftwood.

Sometimes at a construction site you can find wood scraps in the dumpster; those pieces of wood that have not been used will be glad of your care.

Even discarded branches, when remembered as a loom, are made new again. Wherever you live, wherever you are, the makings for a loom are close at hand.

This practical framework for weaving is, as we will explore, also a framework for refocusing our awareness in order to transform how we envision our lives.

When I first put my loom together, out in the woods or on the beach or in my studio, I hold it up and look through the empty rectangle of the loom. I ask myself, "What do you see?" I try to describe to myself, in as much detail as possible, what is pictured in that frame. This is a microcosm of my world, a way to reveal my beliefs to myself. What I believe about that scene is a fractal reflection of my larger view. If I can practice awareness in this tiny window of life, it initiates my awareness of greater truths about what I am and what I do.

I see each stick on the Journey Loom representing an aspect of myself. The whole loom is a metaphor for the structure of my life, like the bones of my body, which, when bound together, make a skeleton with which to move forward. To me, each stick is one aspect of a framework of truth.

Everything that is created arises from the meeting of opposites. Otherwise we are in a state of oneness. Thus the structure of the loom and weaving itself represent in a finite form, the parameters of life. In northern Africa, the vertical axis of the loom is called "axis of the sky" and the horizontal axis is called, "axis of the earth."[3]

It is the thread crossings, the warp in tension and the weft making its way through it that make the fabric possible. The opposite ways of being united in a single web create the whole fabric on the loom, and the whole fabric of the self.

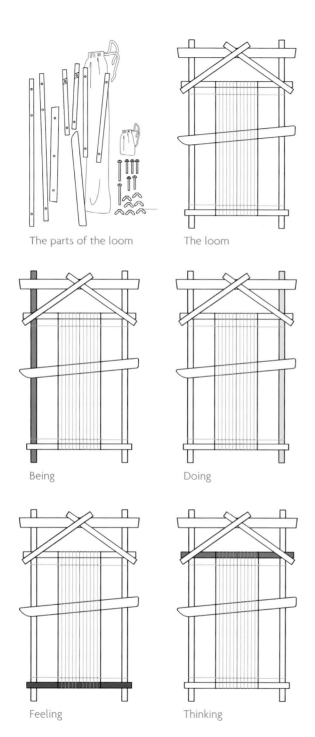

The parts of the loom

The loom

Being

Doing

Feeling

Thinking

The Loom is a metaphor for the structure of life.

The seven sticks of the Weaving a Life loom represent seven aspects of living in our bodies.

The Being and Doing Sticks are the edges of our lives. Stillness (being) and action (doing) are two modes of outer life. They are motivated by our thoughts and feelings; the Being and Doing Sticks separate the Feeling and Thinking Sticks, but connect them as well.

The Listening and Talking Sticks express two modes of verbal communication. Listening requires stillness; Talking requires action.

Listening is a kind of Being and Talking is a kind of Doing, so the Listening and Being Stick connects to the Talking and Doing Stick. The two connect to each other at a single point.

The loom is constructed in three pairs, with the seventh stick as the culmination of the whole structure.

It connects listening and talking to being and doing to thinking and feeling and creates a single point of connection at the top from which stability radiates down into the whole.

The Feeling Stick is the root stick, my grounding stick. It is the basis on which I will begin to weave my life. The Thinking Stick is the upper member of the pair. Feelings and thoughts are two primary modes of our inner life. Each plays into the other.

The Thinking Stick is set apart, yet parallel to the feeling stick, and the warp wound between the two forms the energetic circuit upon which my life as a whole is woven. If the Feeling Stick is at the root or foot, then the Thinking Stick is at the heart of the loom.

My loom forms a gateway into experiencing myself holistically, to re-identify myself as I truly am, myself as more than the sum of my parts. The Listening and Talking Sticks cross each other at a single point on the Creator Stick. My loom is a tool with which I create a potential reality so that I can think/feel, listen/talk to my life before playing it out in the field of doing and being.

The Creator Stick is my connection at the top from which stability and peace radiate down into my whole life. With the Creator Stick, the whole structure becomes a house for the inner warp, as my body is a house for the inner life. With the strength of each stick, we have the solid framework we need to weave thread by thread, moving back and forth between being and doing, building toward the center of our self as Creator and the awareness of our Creator as our self.

The Warp is formed in the energy field between Thinking and Feeling. Life is made of the daily actions woven on the vertical framework of our most sacred values and beliefs. Feeling and Thinking, Being and Doing are woven together in the matrix of the Self. The patterns of our lives are visible in the fabric of our daily actions, built thread by thread.

The Batten is a teacher not connected to my loom but used constantly in the weaving on it. The Batten is the instrument of choice. In the Navaho tradition, the batten is handed down from grandmother to granddaughter as a sacred tool. With the Batten you create your pattern by choosing the threads of the warp you will lift, or the threads of your life that you will follow. These choices will produce your beautiful weaving like a flower from your hands.

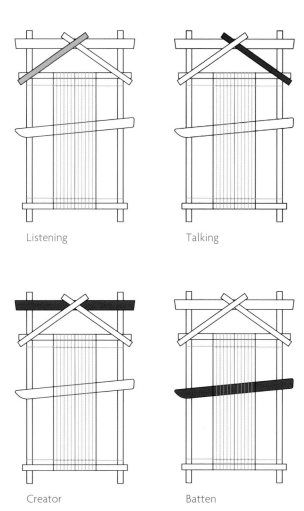

Listening

Talking

Creator

Batten

CHAPTER 4

WARP: INTENTION

Strings of an instrument can be played upon
when tuned with the ear of the musician.
Strings of the warp can be woven upon
when tuned to the touch of the weaver.

Several years ago I met Hernan, a Peruvian *curandero* or shaman, who taught me a great lesson about inner vitality and the art of weaving a life. He told me, "I live most of my life vertically. First I root myself into the earth and I feel this energy and I let it rise straight up through me, my feet, legs, body and my head until it reaches my Creator and I connect with my Creator. That is my vertical life where I do all my work, on the inside just between me and my Creator. When I want to relate to people, I always come from a place of fullness because I have done my inner work. Now I can go to my heart and give away love. How I am in the world, how I appear to you, is my horizontal life."[1]

Our story is a tapestry of our horizontal life. The warp threads are covered so you can see the design, but the warp is where the real work is begun. The warp is our inner life, the vertical inner beliefs we hold.

The warp: vertical threads in tension, our intentions. Careful preparation of the warp threads is the basis for a weaving that will remain strong throughout the process. Much like the strings on a harp, the warp is tuned, each piece of yarn evenly tensioned to the others, until it sings as you run your hand across it.

Attention to making a beautiful, strong, even warp is like the creation of intentions that match our values. Even though you will not see these warp threads in the finished piece, they are the inner strength of the weaving. Each keyform is a guide to gaining an awareness of the structures of our inner life. Each one is designed to impart a distinctive experience, kindling an opportunity to change the viewpoint of your story and how you see the inner journey.

The Threads of the Warp

The first thread on the warp is red. It is the center thread. With this thread, you will always be able to find your way back to your center. The word *Zati* is related to the Urdu word *jath*. *Jath* is the axis of a wheel in a mill; it is also the post that is placed in the center of a cistern or tank to mark its dedication to a deity. The center post marks the recognition of our connection to our Creator.

Red is the color of life. The center thread is your core truth alongside which all other values lie. When you lay the red thread in place and pull it tight, what is it that you know in your deepest heart is true? What great truth drives everything you know? This is your own center thread.

The center thread on the loom identifies the center of our weaving, and reminds us how to find our center, how to return to awareness of our central truth within. Each time the weft passes through the red thread it will remind us to center ourselves. This thread holds the vitality of your weaving, as your vitality arises from the stillness of your center.

What other values do you know are true? How do they relate to the central truth? These are the other warp threads, which lie alongside the central thread, sharing and building on its strength. What are the values out on the edges of your life, the ones that connect you to others and to the world? These will be your selvedges, your relationships, the boundaries between yourself and others.

Weaving a life is the art of looking behind the backdrop of our drama, the weft being acted out on the world stage, and paying attention to the warp, to ourselves as weavers, creators of our story. We are made of many threads, most of which are hidden from view.

As you weave, you will remember the qualities or intentions in the strength of your inner warp, your vertical threads. What you are capable of imagining, you are capable of becoming. If you want to create what you value, practice holding your attention on it.

> "Clear thinking takes us deeper in the practice of meditation. Once the thought waves are stilled, our soul experiences a higher reality through its faculty of direct perception. With our shifting mind anchored, we perceive things and remain unaffected by them, so that we are able to let life go its own way."[2]

The soul has the ability for direct perception; the mind can only repeat what it knows. This ability of the soul is accessible to us through attention to our vertical life.

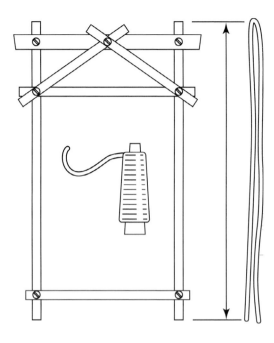

Warping the Seven-Stick Journey Loom

Choosing the Warp Yarn

The warp yarn you choose should be very strong, smooth, and evenly spun with little elasticity. In order for the weft to cover the warp when weaving, warp yarn should be thinner than the yarn you chose for the weft. Cotton and linen are excellent for warp yarns. Although wool is usually more elastic than cotton or linen, you may use wool for warp as long as it is very tightly spun.

Preparing the Warp Yarn

The length and number of warp yarns required for each keyform in this book are listed at the beginning of the instructions for the individual keyforms. After you have chosen your weaving, cut to length the required number of warp yarns.

Warping the Loom

The warp yarns are tied onto the seven-stick Journey Loom using a tapestry warping technique. This technique allows you to easily re-adjust the tension on individual warp yarns as you weave. Most weavings in this book use double warp yarns, but this warping technique also allows you to weave on single warp yarns if a finer weave is desired.

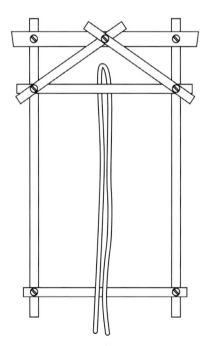

Tying on the Warp

After cutting the required number of warp yarns to the specified length, fold your red centering warp yarn in half. One end will have two loose ends, the other end will form a loop. Take the loop end and place it under the top stick of your loom, with the loose ends hanging down (Step 1, right).

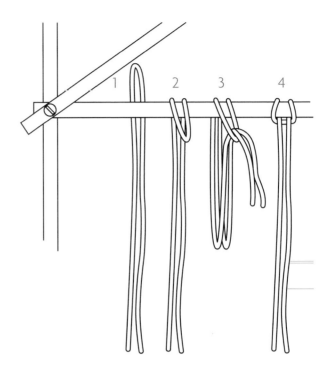

Bring the loop over the top stick to the front (Step 2) and pass the two loose ends through the loop (Step 3).

Pull the two loose ends and tighten the warp onto the stick (Step 4). The loop should be snug and the two loose ends should be hanging down. This knot is known as a "lark's head."

Next, take the two loose warp ends (making sure they are parallel to each other and do not cross) and place them on the front of the bottom stick of your loom.

Bring them around the bottom of the stick to the back side of the loom (Step 5). Separate the two ends and bring the right one up along the right side of the warp yarns, and the left one up along the left side of the warp yarns to the front of the stick (Step 6).

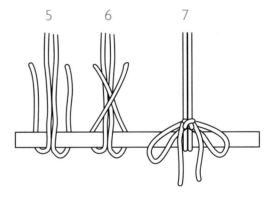

Tie the two ends together in a single knot over the top of the warp yarns (Step 7).

Gently pull up the two ends to tighten the knot and remove any slack from the warp yarn. The warp should be tight like a harp string. When you have tightened the warp yarn to a nice tension, tie the two ends in a bow. Continue to tie on the rest of your warp yarns in this manner, having an equal number of warp yarns on each side of your red centering warp.

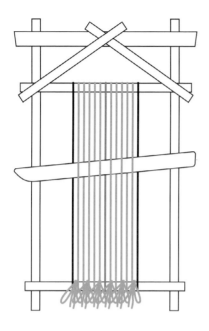

Adjusting the Warp Spacing

After you have tied on all your warp yarns you can adjust the spacing so your weaving will be even. Spacing suggestions are given in the directions for each keyform. To adjust the spacing, begin with either the left or right edge warp and line it up parallel to the side of your loom. Slide the next warp yarn along the top and bottom sticks to the desired distance from the first warp yarn (i.e., ¼ inch).

Repeat with all the other warp yarns. You can check your spacing by measuring the number of warp yarns in one inch

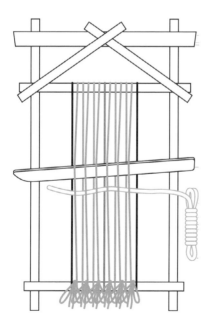

If any warp yarns are too loose, you can untie them and re-tighten them. All the warp yarns should be equal in tension. Try to make any adjustments to the tension before you begin weaving. Your loom is now warped and ready for you to begin.

Note: If you are using a notebook to weave, don't cut the warp in pieces. Wrap as many turns of warp around the notebook as you will need to make it as wide as you want it. Depending on the weight of the warp yarn, the threads will be spaced about ¼ inch apart. Tie the ends together at the back of the notebook. Add one red thread in the middle of the warp, tying it to itself at the back. Slide a pencil or pen under the warp at top and bottom and use a ruler for a batten (see photo of notebook on page 14).

Navaho woman at her loom, c. 1960.
From the author's collection.

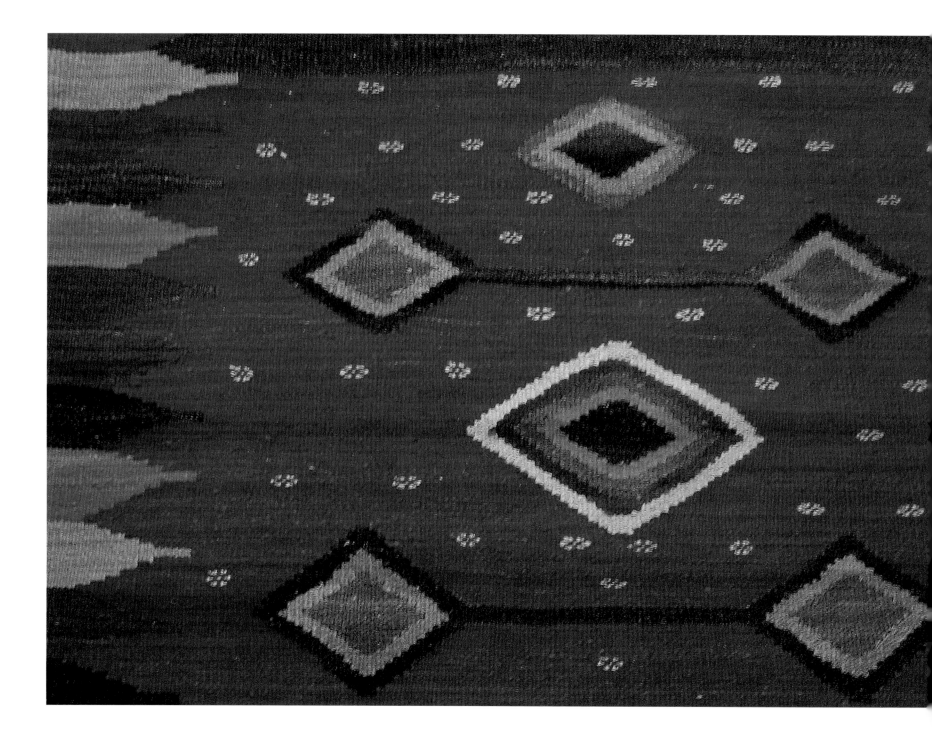

CHAPTER 5

WEAVING: INTEGRATION

*"Weaving involves crossing two threads, the warp and the weft, one vertical
and the other horizontal, one stretched taut and the other undulating and intertwined
with the first. To produce the textile it is necessary for these two threads to be bound,
otherwise each will remain a fragile and fluttering potentiality…
if the meeting of opposites does not take place, nothing is created,
for each element is defined by its opposite and takes its meaning from it."[1]*

The art of weaving is a profound metaphor for understanding the workings of the universe and our place in it. Through the physical process of weaving, we gain a better understanding of this world and how we as human beings are woven into it.

We are bound to our bodies with the fragile threads of earth. Our skeleton is a loom on which every system is strung and woven with our blood. The meeting of opposite elements woven into a whole is the quest of every spiritual seeker. No wonder the art of weaving is so appealing: it is the essential art of creating the unified one out of two opposites.

Archaeological findings suggest that weaving is at least 20,000 years old. But because weavings are so organic and biodegradable, no physical evidence this old has been obtained. The conclusion that weaving is a practice of such antiquity was reached by piecing together clay patterns and paintings with scraps of materials dating back to 5000 BCE.[2]

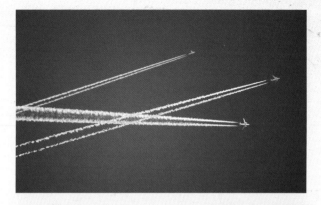

Today we are weaving on the sky through which the space shuttle draws a thread of smoke. A computer is a loom of sorts, weaving a web of information on the grid of pixels and energy across the world.

Weaving has come down through the centuries as a woman's art. Women, who stayed home to take care of the hearth and child could start and stop their spinning and weaving at any time. Thus the distaff, the staff which holds fibers for spinning, symbolizes the women's side of the family. Connected with the ancient goddess cultures, weaving is at the center of creation as personified by the three fates (the old women weavers of Greek mythology), Clotho, who spins us into being, Lachesis, who weaves our fate, and Atropos, who in the end cuts the thread of our lives.

Because I realize my life could end at any time, I work to stay conscious of weaving my daily actions with that which I have deemed valuable. What a hero's journey it is to stay awake to what is valuable! "Our lives reflect our priorities. Our actions speak louder than our words, for everything we do is done in accordance with our priorities. By our actions we determine our top priority."[3]

The weft is built thread by thread, weaving in and out between the warp threads, touching each one as it passes by; in the same way our daily actions weave through our values, touching each one on the way. Weave your threads in, remembering your values as you touch them and lift them to guide the weft threads through. Notice that with every little thread, you touch all your values one by one as you weave a row. This is ultimately all there is to a conscious life. This is how you integrate your life: you touch your values one by one as you guide your actions back and forth to build the fabric of your day.

So how do your daily tasks touch your values? What parts of your life seem to miss them each time? How could you bring your threads back to touch your values?

Bringing them back brings us back to the selvedge, the edge of the weaving. Our selvedges are the self-edges of our lives. Each time you guide the thread through the warp, you reach the outer edge, and you turn the thread back into the warp. Each action you take with your values in mind, each daily task done with your inner structure as its reference, reaches the edge and turns back.

It is this turning back, this rhythm of turning, and turning, and turning that gives your cloth its strength; watch the edges: they will tell you where you are. If you are concentrating on the actions only, and forgetting the vertical strands of values, you will tend to pull them tighter, pulling the warp threads together, and even possibly pulling your values out of line. If you forget to turn back, and forget the values for a while, you may skip some warp threads, and find loose places and uneven edges in your life. This is all part of the natural way! None of us is perfect: our fabric, our process isn't perfect. We are not here to judge, only to learn.

Turning back, turning and turning is like a dance that you learn over time, getting the tension too tight and too loose, and eventually seeing the pattern in your life. Patterns are created when our actions follow rhythms and cycle through the rhythms the way we cycle through our days. We wake, eat, work, rest; these make the stripes and textures of our fabric.

Some love the regularity of stripes of color; some work better without a regular pattern, letting the days come as they will, weaving through their values as they feel right, making a randomly beautiful fabric that is every bit as strong as patterned fabric. Each life is different; each fabric is made of its own threads, even to the individual thread crossings, where intention and action meet. These little moments make the whole, bit by bit as the threads are laid one on the other, day after day until the pattern emerges.

Geri Valentine shares a new handspun, plant-dyed rug with Wednesday Spinners.

Beginnings and endings, emptiness and pattern:

There is a method that intentionally leaves holes in the fabric. Kilim or slit weave leaves holes in a way that keeps the fabric strong. It teaches us that where there are places of loss, where the weft is interrupted, and there is a hole in the fabric of our lives, that fabric is still strong. In the keyform of the mask, we will make the eyes with slit weave. The gap in the fabric becomes an opening through which to see from another perspective. In our woven lives, the empty spaces are the very places where we can see with new eyes, where we can look behind the day-to-day weaving for a moment to see our deeper truths within.

Our imagination is boundless, but we are not alone in the adventure. Even animals—birds, spiders, and beavers—are weavers. And the weavers through the ages who have woven the fabric of history are with us in this moment.

> "Furthermore, we have not even to risk the adventure alone; for the heroes of all time have gone before us; the labyrinth is thoroughly known; we have only to follow the thread of the hero's path. And where we had thought to find an abomination, we shall find a God; where we had thought to slay another, we shall slay ourselves; where we had thought to travel outward, we shall come to the center of our own existence; where we had thought to be alone, we shall be with all the world."[5]

TOP LEFT: Sarah Christie with volunteer at the first EarthLoom, a community weave-in at the Common Ground Fair, Windsor, Maine, 2005.

TOP RIGHT: Wednesday Spinner Kate Henry finishes off the community weaving, "Red Bob and a Thousand Happy Hands," woven by children, adults with disabilities, and every fairgoer who wanted to weave.

BOTTOM LEFT: Many willing hands weave stalks, leaves and branches from their school garden project into an EarthLoom at Troy Howard Middle School in Belfast, Maine.

BOTTOM RIGHT: Children weaving on a Story Loom, a smaller version of the EarthLoom, at the Common Ground Fair in 2006.

Introducing the Cocoon

Tapestry weavers keep yarn ends from dangling by looping the yarn end several times and tying it in the middle. This falls apart if you use it like a shuttle. The "cocoon" is my alternative—a dense cylinder of yarn that acts like a shuttle in hand weaving. The cocoon keeps yarn ends from dangling, allows long lengths, reducing the number of ends, and can be used as a shuttle.

Begin by winding several loops of yarn around your fingers. This is how you do it if you're left handed. Right-handers just reverse the hands.

Pinch the bunch near the end and begin winding the free end around the loops.

Wind the yarn tightly, holding the bundle of loops firmly.

Make the first layer of windings as tight as you can.

Finish the first layer by winding firmly to the other end of the bundle.

Begin adding layers, winding closely from end to end. Keep the cocoon tightly wound and it will work beautifully.

When you have enough yarn cut the end. The cocoon will hang from its yarn end without unwinding.

For shorter lengths of yarn, Weaving a Life Shuttle Cards may be used to pass the weft through the warp.

Instructions: Weaving

The following diagrams will show you how to weave. The basic structures of the weavings on this loom are tapestries. This means that the horizontal weft threads cover the vertical warp threads like this:

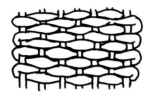

It also means the threads may not go all the way across the warp, but may go only part way for one or several rows to create a design.

To start weaving, pick up your batten stick (one with no holes and a beveled rounded end) and put it under the first edge thread. This is called the selvedge thread (self-edge).

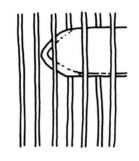

Use the pointed end of the batten stick to lift the first thread. Now slide it over the next thread, under the next one, over, under, until you reach the other selvedge edge.

Turn the batten stick on its side. You will find it raises every other thread, creating a space between the two layers of alternating threads. This is called a "shed."

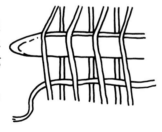

Mayan weavers call the shed the "mouth" of the loom.

Cut a piece of yarn as long as the width of your spread arms. Make a "cocoon" with it if you like.

Pull the yarn through the shed, leaving about a one inch tail.

Remove the batten. Notice that you are already weaving! The next step is to hold the batten in the other hand. Ask yourself "does the weft yarn cross over or under the last thread?" If it went over, you now go under. If it went under, you go over. Always do the opposite of what you did in the last shed, so your weaving will alternate regularly. You will ask yourself the "over or under?" question each time you slide the batten between the threads to open the loom's mouth.

You will see that first you go under-over-under, then you go over-under-over. As you turn the batten on its side to open the mouth of the loom, you can see there are really two possible mouths. When one is open, the other is closed.

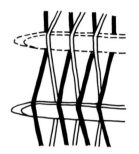

One way to keep the selvedges from pulling in is to build a little slack into each row of weft. You do this by angling the weft. Weave the weft row across at an angle, and push it down with the batten stick. As it goes, it's a little longer than the width of the warp, so it leaves a little slack at the selvedge. It turns out this is just enough to keep the edges straight. You still need to keep an eye on it, but this gives you a way to control the selvedges.

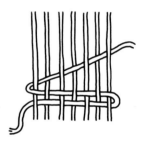

You are weaving! Your only work now is to go back and forth from left to right and right to left. When you want to change colors, fold the end of the color you are working with back in the next shed before you weave in that shed with the second color. When you begin with the second color, leave a one-inch tail and fold it back in the next shed before you weave in that shed. The ends will be covered up in the weaving.

To finish the weaving, take the loom sticks off, slide them out or cut the warp threads from them, and make fringe or knots, or needle the warp ends in. Each of the keyform chapters that follow will teach you more about weaving.

THE KEYFORMS

CHAPTER 6

THE AMULET: INVOCATION

The materials of the amulet are small; it is the intention
of the creator woven into those threads that gives it power to help us
remember our sacred center.

A few years ago I gave a workshop created by Susanne Grosjean and myself, called "The Color Red," at Schoodic Arts for All, an arts festival on the Maine coast. In an open tent on an August day, twenty women gathered to learn something about weaving and natural dyeing and to create an amulet. The experiences in this workshop crystallized my exploration of essential, one might say archetypal, forms of created objects that apply to one's whole life. What evolved for me was a vision of this series of woven forms which could be used as tools for energetic healing. Such forms would call to the psyche to create changes in our awareness of life patterns.

Each woman brought with her an event or condition in need of positive change. Where words cannot reach the healing, a symbol can often reach around and behind the thoughts to a deeper wisdom located like hidden treasure beneath the traps of our literal minds.

Amulets are just such mythic symbols designed, as we now say, to reach the imagery centers of the right hemisphere of the brain. Their purpose is ancient, universal, and appropriate as a language in our time, which we learn to speak with our hearts to the spirit within and every cell in our bodies.

In the workshop, we concentrated with our hands on feeling the textures of natural fibers, choosing by feel the color, pattern, design, light and shadow, tension, edges, and flow. The amulet's purpose is energetically released into being through the kinesthetic handling of the materials and the holding of its intention in the heart. As I have learned, all cultures throughout history have found comfort in this channel to remembering what it means to feel safe and loved.

We talked as we wove, sometimes singing, in the ancient ritual of women working together, freed to go deep into our intuitive place of creative work, stirring the present moment into a deep breathing together.

All over the world people create amulets for the same reasons: to call for help in changing the nature of how we experience our lives. They are an invocation of a power greater than ourselves to bless what is good in our lives.

The sacred pollen pouch of the Navaho contains corn pollen, the essence of life and growth, with which traditional Navahos bless each new day.

In central Asia, an amulet is hung over the cradle of the newborn because it can not yet protect itself. The motifs most chosen for protection and encoded into the fabric of weavers have been the bird (an ancient goddess symbol intended to mediate between this world and the world of the spirits), the horns of the ram, elk, and deer, as well as plants, flowers, and trees. The axis mundi is called the "tree of life" pattern because it reaches from below the earth and into heaven, covering all dimensions of life. Words from a sacred text are often written on paper or cloth and sewn inside the weaving to be worn close to the heart.[1]

Developmentally, the amulet represents conception, the spark of becoming.

When you perceive that you have something of value, the longing to protect it follows closely. The amulet becomes an outer manifestation of this perception and this longing. It signifies the transforming of fear of loss into the awareness of wholeness, and the loving act of protection. Traditionally, an amulet is an object imbued with power to ward off negative energy.

Amulets are often made of weavings because the weaver's intention is a part of its creation. It's something to touch, to remember, to encourage our daily actions with the light of our beliefs. It lets us remember that our lives have value, that what we value is important, and that the structure of our life is built on our values. The amulet is a safe place to receive and keep this information for remembrance. It awakens the sleepwalking of unconscious action to an awareness that our life is built on love and a sense of wholeness, on the things we hold most true.

The materials of the amulet are small; it is the intention of the creator woven into those threads that gives it power to help us remember our sacred center.

By the end of the second day, we sat in a circle around the red cloth and each shared our story and the meaning of our amulet to us. This simple exploration had a deeply unifying effect. The weaving itself created a sense of unification for each participant. From cancer to abuse, to coming out as a person who is gay, to having a child, each woman expressed her intention to heal their separation from their Self with new vision.

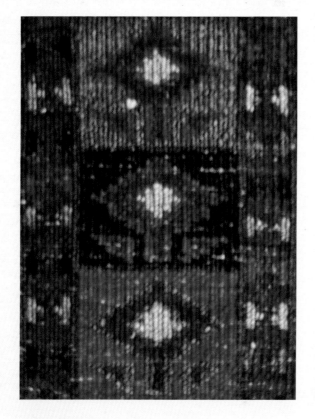

Carefully chosen yarns, resonant colors woven on the frame looms and embellished with ribbon, beads and shells, made lovingly with their own hands in their own time, this bit of cloth became valuable. Much like our body, made of similar elements, which can be experienced at a deeper level as we take time to create a hand-made life.

As we completed the circle, we were all in tears. We were witness for each other and of the power inherent in our longing for grace embodied in this bit of cloth each of us had woven. We saw that it was within our power to call for help with the work of weaving a life. Each of us saw clearly that the object itself was not powerful, but was imbued with power. The power was in our intention to remember and nurture our truest Selves.

KEYFORMS: *The Amulet*

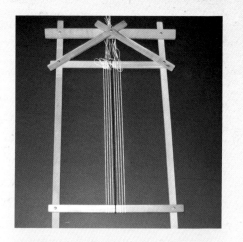

Warping the Loom

To make your amulet begin with 9 warp yarns that are 62 inches long. Tie these 9 warp yarns onto the loom with the tie at the top warp stick of the loom, and the "lark's head" loops at the bottom. (See pages 22–24 for directions on warping the loom.) Space the pairs of warp yarns ¼ inch apart (4 pairs per inch).

Weaving the Amulet

Begin weaving approximately two inches from the bottom warp stick of your loom. Weave your batten over and under pairs of warp threads, opening a shed as shown on page 33. You may begin from either side. Starting your weaving near the bottom of the loom will allow enough length of unwoven warp to make the necklace portion of your amulet.

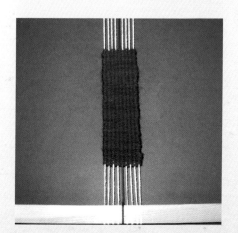

Weave until the piece measures 5 inches long. Work in all your weft ends with a tapestry yarn needle or darning needle.

Finishing the Amulet

Now you are ready to take your weaving off the loom. Begin by untying the first 5 warp pairs (10 ends) from the top warp stick of the loom. Separate the two red warp threads, and bundle one with the other warp ends to the right. Gather the threads and tie them in an overhand knot as close to the weaving as you can. You will have long tails free for braiding or twisting.

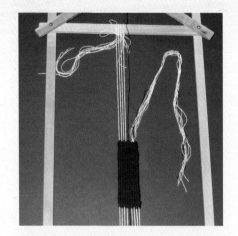

Gather the remaining warp ends and tie them in an overhand knot to match.

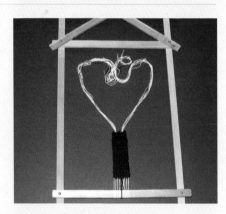

It is easier to braid the necklace part of the amulet while it is still attached to the loom. Begin by dividing one side of the necklace warp (4 pairs plus one of the red threads) into 3 strands for braiding. There will be three warp ends in each strand. Braid these three strands together to form the necklace of the amulet. If you wish to add beads to the necklace you can string them onto one of the warp yarns as you braid. Repeat with the other side and tie the two braided strands together to form the necklace.

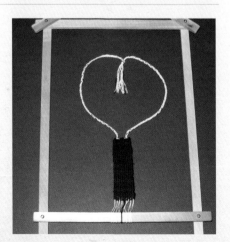

You will want the bottom warp ends of the amulet to be as long as possible for tying off and working in. With sharp pointed scissors gently lift the loop end of the warp yarn where it crosses itself, up and away from the warp, and cut it, being careful not to cut into the weaving. You want to cut only the loop of the warp yarn.

Finish the warp ends by tying two warp pairs together with an overhand knot (two pairs of warp ends in each knot). When you get to the middle you will need to add one red warp thread to its neighboring pair. To "hide" the warp ends, use your tapestry needle to thread the ends of your warps a half inch or so into the back of the weft parellel to the warp. If you would like to leave the ends free for embellishment you can thread the warp ends under just the first two or three rows of weaving on the front of the fabric (what will become the outside of the amulet), leaving the ends to hang down for a fringe, and knotting them or stringing on beads.

To finish the amulet, fold the weaving in half from bottom to top. Beginning at the top edge, sew down one side of the amulet with a tapestry needle and yarn. At the bottom folded edge, thread the sewing yarn through the weaving on the inside of the amulet to the other bottom corner. Continue sewing up the other side. Thread your sewing yarn end back into the edge of the weaving a half inch or so, and trim any excess.

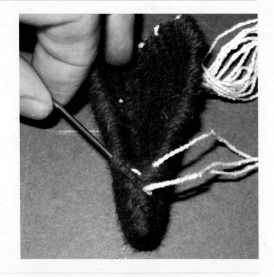

Embellish your amulet with beads, shells, tiny bells, your grandmother's buttons, or any small objects that mean something to you and add to your intention for your amulet.

CHAPTER 7

THE RECEIVING BOWL: INVITATION

"Come creators
Come designers of life
Step into the light
The circle of your
Sacred Self
With tenderness and joy"[1]

When a newborn child comes into our life, we feel the joy and the mystery wrapped up in one experience. We can't help feeling love for this new form, holding it in a receiving blanket, protecting it with our life without reservation or condition. How can we turn this kind of love toward ourselves?

As I grew up, I learned to be scanning always for what was wrong with me. In my work, I have discovered that most of us are still doing this. The receiving bowl represents the stage of new birth in our life, in which we daily change our viewpoint on ourselves.

The receiving bowl is an invitation to explore what we believe about ourselves with fresh eyes. Our experience of love in our lives does not have to depend on our circumstances or our life story. It is based on our choice to nurture it and grow it and weave it into this present moment.

The receiving bowl is a flat two-dimensional weaving until you take it off the loom and pull the warp threads together, reshaping it to make a seamless and beautiful bowl. This is exactly what we can do with our beliefs: take the flat, empty places, the reactive, "what's wrong" life, the choices that hold nothing for us, and find our conscious intentions. We can pull on them, applying their force to reshape our beliefs into a vessel for our true selves.

This journey is to seek out the positive, to nurture ourselves, embrace ourselves, forgive ourselves. What if the purpose of life is to develop an intimate relationship with yourself and learn the truth about love?

The bowl recognizes that to want to discover the wholeness of the universe is a worthwhile endeavor. The bowl begins with actions that seem to make no sense. They're different from daily actions. They have an odd shape, and leave gaps where we usually fill in. Allowing oneself to take the irrational steps to discover that which is beyond the rational is the experience of the bowl. Developmentally, this leap from familiar comfort into the unknown is the keyform of birth.

The bowl is woven in curves, leaving large areas of empty warp threads. What happened to our regular patterns and the rhythm of turning back and back? With the bowl, the values remain very visible, but you create a new rhythm.

Taking the leap to begin the investigation of that which makes no rational sense has been called a "leap of faith." But what is faith? It is not a set of ideas given by a group or another person. It is not precepts followed blindly. Faith is that which you instinctively, in your most interior place, hold to be true. It is that which you know in your very bones to be true, so that you don't have to consider it or question it because you know it's true. You don't have to think about it—you live it.

But where does faith come from? We can embark on a new belief by taking it as a working hypothesis. Just try it on, follow it to its conclusion, and see how it holds up. Those things we have experienced deeply and fully in our lives have held up as we followed their threads out to the end. This is faith.

So we take this leap of faith, this acceptance of trying something new. We take the pattern of strange shapes that are the foundation of the bowl as a working hypothesis, and wonder what we will find. Five small shapes in a sea of space create the bowl. The secret is in the space: get to know the empty places.

Pull on the warp threads, and the shapes draw together into something new and unexpected: they take on depth and dimension! Pull on what you love, drawing your life into a new shape. Now you can become a vessel to receive a new view of yourself.

In embarking on a journey to find a greater truth than that of the world of our sensory experiences, we give ourselves permission to receive something unknown. When we look at the bowl, splayed on the loom, from our previous experience, it looks silly and wrong. The lives of those seeking spiritual truths often look silly and wrong from the outside. We have our own truths to live with and live on, and to live out. The bowl is a vessel to hold and to serve to us something greater than our daily image of ourselves.

The bowl has an inside and an outside. Every choice we make has an inner motive and an outer action. Is it the shape of the inside of the bowl that makes the outside? Or the other way around? Our inner life is protected within the vessel of the body. We touch the inner world with the experiences of our past and what we have come to believe about ourselves. We touch the outer world with our bodies, our hands, our skin, our eyes and ears, our thoughts.

All the deep beliefs we have about ourselves create the forms of our outer experience. How can we ever get to loving ourselves? We have to grow new beliefs.

One who creates chooses what will be part of the creation and what will not be part of the creation. This power is not in what is around you, not in what others believe, but in what you believe about yourself.

In this life we can learn to receive ourselves with our whole hearts. We have the choice to accept ourselves with compassion and wonder. If we choose to welcome who we are in new each moment, we can quiet our judgment and stand in awe of the mysterious phenomenon of our body, mind, and spirit. With the hands of our beliefs laid with love on our daily lives, every single detail of life, just the way it is, without condition or qualification, can be pure bliss.

Let every cell of your body know how much you accept it, love it and are willing to ride the waves no matter how rough the sea. By honoring, caring, and treating yourself with respect, you come to a truth about who you really are.

> This is the secret of the receiving bowl:
> What you believe is what you receive.

Be grateful for your life, every detail of it, and your face will come to shine like a sun, and everyone who sees it will be made glad and peaceful. Persist in gratitude, and you will slowly become one with the Sun of Love and Love will shine through you its all-healing joy. This path of gratitude is not for children: it is the path of tender heroes, of heroes of tenderness who, what ever happens, keep burning on the altar of their hearts the flame of adoration.

— Rumi[2]

INSTRUCTIONS: *The Receiving Bowl*

Warping the Loom

To make the receiving bowl, begin with 25 warp yarns that are 54 inches long. Tie these 25 warp yarns onto the loom with the tie at the bottom warp stick, creating 25 warp pairs. See pages 22–24 for directions on warping the loom. Space the warp pairs ¼ inch apart or 4 ends per inch.

Twining the Edge

Beginning with a row of twining will make a firmer edge at the top of your bowl. With your weft cocoon or shuttle card, tie the end of your weft to the right vertical stick of the loom. Pass the weft yarn under the warp pairs and around the left vertical stick. Beginning at the first warp pair on either edge, pass the weft yarn over the warp and over and around the weft yarn that is behind the warps. You will have twisted the top weft yarn over the bottom weft yarn once between the first and second warp pairs.

Continue to pass the weft over the next warp pair and around the stationary weft yarn behind the warps until you have twisted the two weft yarns together between all the warp pairs. Be careful not to pull too tightly on the weft as you twine to avoid distorting the warp spacing. When you are finished you should have a single line of weft that wraps in and out of the warps with a twist in between each warp pair.

Weaving the Bowl

The receiving bowl is a perfect example of the Zati weaving technique. It is woven as five leaf shapes using the plain weave shown on pages 32 and 33. Unwoven warp yarns are left exposed between the leaves. After the bowl is taken off the loom, you will be pulling the warp yarns to join the leaves together, creating a three-dimensional bowl shape.

Beginning at one warp edge (these directions begin from the right), pick up the first and then every other warp (odd-numbered) with your batten omitting the last 6 warp pairs; they will not be woven in this shed. Using the shuttle card or weft cocoon, wrap it once around the stationary weft yarn and place it into the first shed. You can leave the stationary weft end tied to the loom until you have finished weaving.

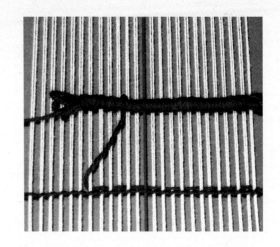

To pick up the second shed, beginning at the left warp edge, omit the first six warp yarns and pick up the alternate warp yarns from the previous shed, again omitting the last six warp yarns. You will be weaving on only the middle 13 warp yarns in this shed with six unwoven warps on each side. This begins the first leaf shape.

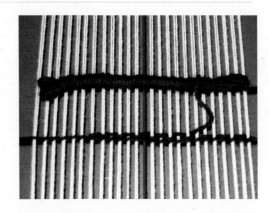

To create the first leaf shape you will be weaving in alternating sheds and picking up one additional warp pair on the outer edge in each shed as you go until you have only 2 unwoven warp yarns on each side. Your last shed should be 2 unwoven warps, 21 woven warps, 2 unwoven warps.

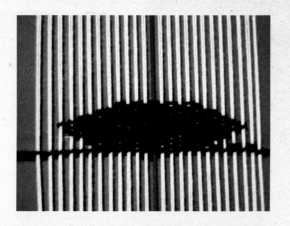

Now you will weave back in toward the center of the bowl by omitting one warp on the outer edge in each shed until you have 9 unwoven warps on each side and only 7 warps woven in the center. This completes the first leaf shape of your bowl.

The second leaf shape will be woven slightly differently from the first leaf. In the next shed weave the 7 middle warps plus one more on the outer edge. Continue weaving in alternating sheds adding one more warp on the outer edge in each shed until you have 3 warps unwoven on each side. In the next shed you will be including 2 additional outer warps instead of one, so you are now left with just 1 unwoven warp on the outer edge. Repeat for the next shed. You should now have 1 unwoven warp on each side and 23 woven warps in the middle.

To finish the second leaf you will be weaving back to the middle. In the next two sheds omit 3 outer warps on the outside edge. Continue to weave in alternating sheds omitting one warp on the outer edge in each shed until you have 9 unwoven warps on each side and 7 woven warps in the middle. This completes the second leaf shape.

To create the middle leaf of the bowl you will once again be weaving to the outer edges picking up one additional warp on the outer edge in each shed. Beginning with the 7 middle warps in the next shed pick up one additional warp on the outer edge. Continue weaving in alternating sheds adding one additional warp on the outer edge in each shed until you have only 2 unwoven warps on each outer edge. In the next shed add these 2 remaining unwoven warps to the shed. Repeat for the next shed. You should now have woven all 25 warps in the last shed.

To finish the middle leaf you will be weaving back to the middle of the bowl. In the next 2 sheds omit 2 warps on each outer edge. Continue weaving in alternating sheds omitting 1 warp on the outer edge in each shed until you have 9 unwoven warps on each outer edge and 7 woven warps in the middle. This completes the middle leaf shape and half of your bowl.

To create the fourth leaf shape you will be repeating the second leaf shape.

In the next shed weave the 7 middle warps plus one more on the outer edge. Continue weaving in alternating sheds adding one more warp on the outer edge in each shed until you have 3 warps unwoven on each side. In the next shed you will be including 2 additional outer warps instead of one, so you are now left with just 1 unwoven warp on the outer edge. Repeat for the next shed. You should now have 1 unwoven warp on each side and 23 woven warps in the middle.

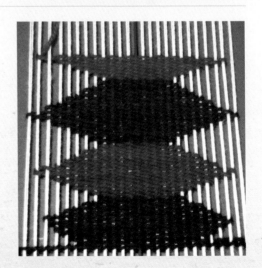

To finish the fourth leaf you will be weaving back to the middle. In the next two sheds omit 2 outer warps on the outside edge. Continue to weave in alternating sheds omitting one warp on the outer edge in each shed until you have 9 unwoven warps on each side and 7 woven warps in the middle. This completes the fourth leaf shape.

To create the fifth and final leaf shape you will be repeating the first leaf shape.

You will be weaving in alternating sheds and picking up one additional warp yarn on the outer edge in each shed until you have only 2 unwoven warp yarns on each side. Your last shed should be 2 unwoven warps, 21 woven warps, 2 unwoven warps.

To finish the last leaf shape you will weave back in toward the center of the bowl by omitting one warp yarn on the outer edge in each shed until you have 6 unwoven warps on each side and 13 warps woven in the center. In the next shed weave across to the outer warp edge. To finish the rim of the bowl repeat the twining that you used for the beginning edge of the weaving. Take the weft yarn around the left vertical stick behind all the warps and around the right vertical stick. With the remaining weft yarn twine over and around each warp and the stationary weft behind the warps. This completes the weaving for your bowl.

Finishing the Receiving Bowl

To remove your bowl from the loom untie the warp yarns from the bottom warp stick.

Beginning with the red centering warp, tie one red warp yarn with its two neighboring warp yarns. Continue to tie the remaining warp yarns together—two at a time—with an overhand knot close to the weaving until all the warps have been tied (12 knots in all).

Next, carefully cut the warps from the top warp stick and the weft yarns from the side sticks and knot them together. Beginning on an outer edge, gently pull on the first warp yarn until the spaces between the leaves begin to close. Working from the outside warps to the middle warps, gently pull on each warp yarn until the spaces between the leaves are completely closed. As you pull the warps the edges of the leaves will come together, creating your bowl.

You may need to adjust the tension on individual warps to smooth out the shape of your bowl. When you have pulled all the warp yarns and shaped the bowl, finish the edge of the bowl. The photos show simply tying the warp yarns together two at a time with an overhand knot close to the weaving, for a decorative edge.

To create a plain edge, sew in all your warp and weft ends. Or you may choose to thread beads or other small objects onto the warp ends.

CHAPTER 8

THE DOLL: INSIGHT

The doll is the symbol of the soul.
It is a small spark of the greater Self.

Instinctively, we know that the doll is a symbol of our inner life. It captures our imagination, whether it is a beautifully detailed figure or a simple bundle of rags. The doll is an imaginal form realized, and carries with it insight into the meaning and nature of our journey.

My friend Geri Valentine says as she holds her Zati doll up to her ear, "this is my self-phone." She told me that as she traveled across the country with her doll, she never got lost. The relationship between you and your doll includes nurturing and friendship. The emergence of personas elicited by the doll includes the child who knows how to trust. We can learn from this child inside us how to allow ourselves to become absorbed in deep and sacred play. Under layers of illusions our true identity is hidden. How can we come to know what shining beings we are? How do we grow that shy little love into a glow that lights up our lives?

When I was a kindergarten teacher in Waldorf schools, the children gave me insight into the power of a relationship with a handmade doll. Each season, we created new dolls out of washed wool, handspun yarn and soft woven cotton fabric to add to our family of dolls. Each one was born with awe and adoration because the doll is a true keyform, an elemental thing that touches us so deeply that it opens our hearts to the nature of relationship. The dolls were the heart of the classroom. They mirrored our actions, hopes, and fears but also our love and feelings of self-worth. As we put them away each afternoon, they were wrapped in their blankets with a lullaby and placed gently in bed to sleep and dream until the next day. The dolls deserved our utmost respect because they held the key to the realm of nourishing play. Developmentally, the doll is the keyform of the freshness and innate wisdom of youth.

The doll begins with a return to the now-familiar weaving of daily actions through the inner value structure we have discovered and disclosed to ourselves. The doll is made of fabric that is now consciously rich in intention and action. It may be patterned or "plain" or freely built, muted or bright. Whether the fabric is wide or narrow, whether the doll is tall or short, the fabric is made of the same pure process, the same inner structure. We don't judge the width of fabric, but we see the love in the daily actions of the threads that built it.

The doll begins with what we suddenly realize is a vessel! The experience of the bowl gave us a demonstration of the experience of another dimension, the inner dimension, and the doll shows us that the body is a vessel for the self. Once we have created this vessel, we stabilize it. The stone in the foot of the doll, millions of years old, steadies and grounds it, allowing it to stand upright. What ancient connection or knowledge steadies you, makes you most grounded and solid? Finding your footing and balance in order to walk your journey is essential for moving forward.

The doll is a vessel, as our bodies are vessels. A vessel has an outside and an inside. The outside makes contact with the outer world, as we touch the doll and play with this being we are creating. The response to the outside begins inside: with what will we fill our doll? Our bodies are vessels made of intention and action: what kind of experiences do we fill ourselves with? What do we take in?

Choose materials that speak to you, that seem most right to become your doll's "self-stuff." You can choose materials that speak to you in your own heart, to choose what fills your own body.

Finishing the doll is a discovery of the ageless wise person within you. How many of us see that we are right now filled with the "right stuff?" We have that wise part of us that knows this is true.

Weaving the Doll

The doll's dress is woven on the seven-stick Journey Loom with colors and designs that tell the story of an emerging future for yourself blossoming into the present.

For myself, I weave mentors; soulful archetypes who carry the vision of my current life as I carry it with me day by day. I imagine peeling off the layers of doubt and illusion I have about myself. I allow myself to be old and beautiful with wonderful grey hair and a belly. Simple contentment is one of my goals, so I weave simple contentment into the texture of her dress. Sometimes I make an apron for her, sometimes a sword. I get to play whatever I want her to be. This gives me insight into what I want to become. I ask myself, "Who am I as an elder, what do I know, what do I value?"

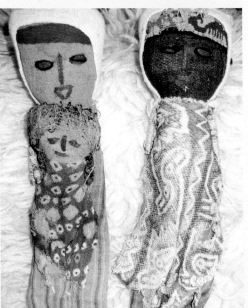

How do you see yourself now, and who you are inside? What are the unseen, undiscovered treasures in you? Use the materials at hand to weave this insight into your doll.

I look in my favorite places—beaches, woods— for the right stone. I place it at the fold of her skirt, then sew up the sides and fill her body with balsam fir needles or lavender, and wisps of wool.

Next I sew on a head to connect with her heart. The head is a little fabric bundle; we recognize our doll even without a face!

The hair is created with raveled yarn, or any interesting bit of wool or fiber. It can be braided or knotted. It could be made of many strands of yarn, bundled and tied, then sewn in place.

Next I braid, twist, or felt arms. Though the instructions show separate arms, I sometimes make them in one piece from shoulder to shoulder with a loose knot in the center so she (or he!) can "hold" something in the hands by slipping it into the knot or through the arms, like the doll at right. Finally, I make a shawl or serape. I knit or crochet or weave a small rectangle or triangle. You may have a piece of cloth from a family member, or a favorite fragment you have been saving.

Sometimes I weave a little basket for my doll to carry. I even ask what she or he wants. This is the insight your doll will help you receive. Your doll will answer you. Ask anything, then…listen!

The keyform of the Doll is the form to help harmonize, balance, guide and nurture you on the journey of weaving your life. The relationship you have with your doll will give you insight about the way you nurture yourself. Playing this way with your future will create a quiet path into your sweet heart and open the door for an unexpected relationship with your shy love.

What does your wise elder know that is still hidden from you? Think of your elder now, powerful and content, loving herself or himself just as they are. Fulfillment comes from the inside, no matter who else or what else is around. Your elder will stay with you while you navigate the dark and come into your own light.

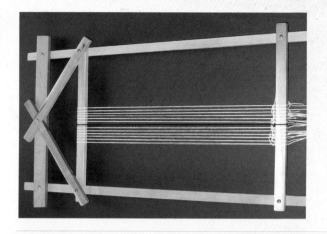

INSTRUCTIONS: *The Doll*

Warping the Loom

To make your doll, begin with 13 warp yarns that are 54 inches long. Tie these 13 warp yarns onto the loom with the tie at the bottom warp stick (see pages 22–24 for directions on warping the loom). Space the warp yarns ¼ inch apart or 4 ends per inch. You will also need a small stone about 1¼ inch in diameter and ½ inch thick. The stone needs one flat face, and is ideally oval or rectangular. You will also need some wool fibers to make a felted ball for the head, or for stuffing a cloth head as well as for stuffing your doll. Find some "hairy" wool or yarn for the hair.

Weaving the Doll

To shape the front neck and shoulders of your doll you will begin weaving with short rows as follows: Skip the first 5 warp pairs at the right warp edge and pick up only the sixth and eighth warps with your batten to create the first shed. Place your weft yarn in this shed. You will be weaving only on the middle 3 warp pairs, skipping 5 warps on each side.

For the second shed, add the seventh and ninth warps. Place your weft yarn in this shed.

Continue picking up and weaving alternating sheds adding one more warp on the outer edge to each shed as you go until you have reached the outer edge warps and have woven all 13 warp pairs.

Weave on all 13 warp yarns until the piece measures 11½ inches.

To shape the back neck and shoulders you will be reversing the shaping for the front that you did at the beginning of the weaving. In the next shed omit one warp yarn from the outer edge. Continue to omit one warp yarn from the outer edge of each shed as you go until you have 5 unwoven warps on each side and only 3 woven warps in the middle.

This completes the weaving for your doll.

To remove the doll from the loom begin by untying the warp yarns from the bottom warp stick of the loom. Tie two adjacent warp pairs (4 ends) together, tying one of the red center warp yarns with each adjacent warp pair to the left and right of the center warp (5 ends) in an overhand knot (total of 6 knots) close to the weaving.

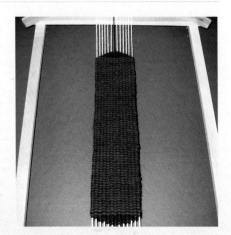

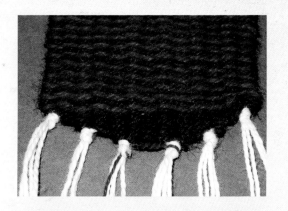

Next, carefully cut the warp ends off the top warp stick of the loom. Tie these warp ends together as before in an overhand knot close to the weaving.

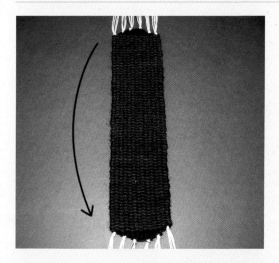

Fold the woven piece in half lengthwise.

Beginning at the top open end on one side, about ¼ inch below the shoulder edge, sew the two edges together down the length of the piece to 1 inch from the bottom folded edge.

To make the base of the doll so she can stand, fold the unsewn 1 inch at the bottom in half perpendicular to the side seam creating a T shape. Sew along this bottom seam.

Repeat the sewing for the other side of the doll by sewing the other two edges together lengthwise (leaving ¼ inch at the top) to within 1 inch of the bottom edge. Fold the bottom perpendicular as above but before sewing the bottom together insert your stone into the bottom of the doll.

Sew up the bottom edge. The stone in the bottom will help to ground your doll so she can stand firmly on her own. Using clean, loose wool fibers, stuff the body of the doll. You may want to include balsam fir needles, lavender, rose petals, or healing/aromatic herbs.

Making Arms for the Doll

The arms for your doll will be made using a simple twisting technique to create a cord. You will need 4 or 5 pieces of weft yarn that are 28 inches long. If you want thicker arms you can add a few more pieces of yarn. Tie the 4 or 5 yarn pieces together with an overhand knot on one end. Hold the knot between your toes (or otherwise secure this end) and holding the other loose ends in your hands, pull the yarn taught and twist the bundle of yarns to the right.

Keep twisting until the yarn bundle tightens and will twist back on itself when you release the tension on the cord.

When there is enough twist in the cord, bring the two ends together and hold them while allowing the cord to twist together. Run your hand down the length of the cord several times to smooth out the twist. You should now have a double twisted cord with a loop on one end where it was folded in half and two loose ends. Tie the two loose ends together with an overhand knot. Trim the ends next to the knot.

Lay the arm cord along the top un-sewn edge of the doll with both ends of the cord hanging out the sides and the middle of the cord inside the weaving. Adjust the side with the knot to the correct length for an arm.

Beginning with one arm, with the side seams on each side of the arm, sew around the arm connecting it to the open sides of the side seam. Tuck the warp ends into the body of the doll and sew across the shoulder and neck of the doll to the other arm. Make sure that the middle of the arm cord is tucked into the body of the doll. (Add additional wool stuffing to fill out the shoulders and neck if needed.) Sew around this arm connecting it to the open sides of the side seams. You will now have the doll body and arms sewn together. Tie the other arm in an overhand knot, adjusting the length to equal the other arm. Trim the ends.

Doll Head and Hair

You will be making a simple felted ball for the head of your doll. Take a small handful of clean loose wool fibers. Gently tease the fibers into a loose ball and gently roll in your hands to form a ball. If you are making a cloth head, there is no need to felt the wool.

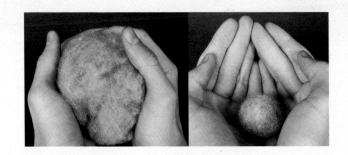

Add a drop or two of dish washing detergent to your ball and soak in hot water until completely wetted. With gentle circular motions roll the wet wool between your hands. The ball will be quite loose to begin with but as the fibers begin to felt together the ball will become firmer. As it begins to come together you can increase the pressure between your hands. Continue to roll and knead the ball between your hands until it is a firm round ball. (You may need to add more detergent and/or hot water as you work.) Rinse the ball under very cold water to finish the felting.

Sew the head ball onto the neck edge of the doll with short stitches. A curved needle will make it easier.

Sew hair onto your doll using either yarn or wool locks. You are now ready to dress and adorn your doll.

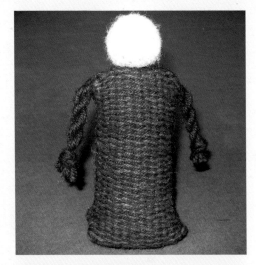

CHAPTER 9

THE BELT OF POWER: CHOICE

*"If I stay in this moment with love, the fear has no place to live. I will use this knife
to cut away any thing that keeps me from my purpose."*[1]

The belt of power is much like the ancient cingulum, a rope encircling the waist, worn by the Akkadian goddess Ishtar, whose Sumerian counterpart was Inanna. The cord is four and a half feet in length with a knot and tassel at the end so it can be used as a compass for the sacred nine foot circle (which was also used in Celtic practices). In Egyptian hieroglyphics, the symbol of an oval cord with a knot in it, around a cartouche or hieroglyphic, indicates the magical power in that name or word.[2]

The keyform of the Belt of Power, with its sheath for your knife or symbol of choice, is the keyform of commitment to your Self. We can learn to cut away from us energy that no longer serves us with the knife of choice; we can choose to encircle our sacred space with the power of our growing love. Developmentally this is the stage of adolescence, of making our own choices.

The Belt of Power offers you the strength of an inner commitment to eliminate what no longer supports your beliefs. Through the ages, the belt of power has signified the ability to cut away the useless and harmful, encircling only the essence of Truth. The knife is the emblem of choice, of cutting the cords that have bound us to the past so that we might strengthen our commitment to embody what we can envision.

> "Firm resolve is the determination to make things happen…When it becomes time for us to do what is important for us to do, we have to use our ego. But the use of the ego is only a faculty, not an identity."[3]

When we become aware of our capacity for choice, we begin to learn how to use our knife with precision. Stepping aside from our identity with our ego, we can direct our human life with spiritual purpose.

The knife on the belt of power is a mythical tool that represents the great sword used in bravery by Amazons, samurai, knights and all archetypes of heroic strength. This is the Keyform to connect to your inner strength with clear thinking.

"In ancient Sanskrit, the mind is considered
to have four functions:
Manas, the part of our mind that notices
Chitti, the part of our mind that remembers
Buddhi, the part of our mind that chooses
Ahankar, the part of our mind that tells our body to go
and get the object of our choice."[4]

Try the experiment of closing your eyes and opening them again. Where has your sight landed? What do you notice? What is in the field of your awareness? (That is Manas.)

Now, what does that awareness mean to you? In other words, what is your association with what you are looking at? (That is Chitti.)

What do you choose to do with that awareness? Buddi is your point of power: the power is in your choice.

What will you do, now that you have chosen? Ahankar comes into play here. You choose, then you act. The slowing down of the process, through the conscious action of weaving, gives you time to consider, to discriminate between what glitters and what is actually gold.

Thoughts and feelings are forms of energy. Negative energy vibrates at low frequencies. It is heavy. Remember how you feel when you are depressed. It drags you down. Positive energy vibrates at higher frequencies. It is light. Remember how you feel when you are vibrant and happy. When we begin to intentionally focus on the positive instead of the negative, we change our lives, add to the lives of those around us and the energy in the world. The core dynamic of the journey of Weaving our Life is the energetic change we are calling into being as we travel the road to loving our Self.

Choosing the negative tends to disintegrate your life. The more angry and greedy you become, the more your self will fall apart. When you embrace and find time for that which creates love in your life, you will integrate and come together. When you choose resentment, it is a choice to create chaos, anger, and depression. You are powerful beyond your wildest dreams.

Every few minutes, life will present us with an opportunity to practice choosing well. When desires look too good to pass up, and we feel that sideways pull reaching its hand toward that thing we would rather not be doing, remember the keyform of the Belt of Power. It will give you the power to face negative energy and say "no" to fear and anger and "yes" to the energy that will lift you and integrate you into being your strong Self.

With the receiving bowl we begin to accept ourselves completely through all the changes as they appear. With the belt of power, we delineate our sacred space, defining an area that is not to be transgressed by anyone. This is the space in which we take the journey, whatever it may be. This is the inner space we give ourselves for the realization of our choices. It may involve designating outer space as well: claiming a room for our work, or building a space, or claiming a time in our busy day that is just for our inner work.

Where do you want to focus your attention? How do you bring forward the thoughts you want to have, and leave aside the thoughts that are not helpful for you now? The process of learning to make the choice can be like taming a feral animal, when our choices have been based more on reactions to events than on an inner vision. Give yourself loving attention at a distance until you can get closer to your heart: heart and mind will get to know and accept each other as allies. It's just a matter of time, patience, and loving attention until the answer you are seeking is revealed by you for every single challenge in your life. You are not only the design but also the designer.

With this keyform you will claim and encircle the truth about yourself and disclaim with clarity what is no longer needed. This is the real work of the Belt of Power. You will weave the sheath for your knife, which is attached to the cord created of many threads and plied into your cincture. As you create the thread crossings of your life, you learn to defend yourself fiercely while remaining in a place of love, to give yourself the time and allow yourself the space to explore what is truly of value to you, and the time and resources to act on those values.

> "We are all sacred beings of light, who have entirely the sufficient amount of power to manifest the life that we want, to create the space in our life that allows us full self-expression, and the full expression of our powers and abilities. That's the truth for all of us, and it's the truth for you."[5]

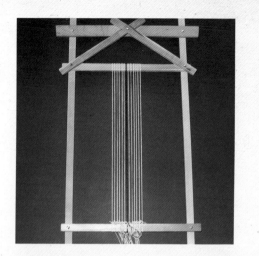

INSTRUCTIONS: *The Belt of Power*

Warping the Loom

To make the sheath for the Belt of Power, begin with 13 warp yarns that are 54 inches long. Tie these 13 warp yarns onto the loom with the tie at the bottom warp stick (See pages 22–24 for directions on warping the loom). Space the warp yarns ¼ inch apart or 4 ends per inch.

Twining the Edge

Beginning with a row of twining will make a firmer edge at the top of your sheath. With your weft cocoon or shuttle card, tie the end of your weft to the right vertical stick of the loom. Pass the weft yarn under the warp pairs and around the left vertical stick. Beginning at the first warp pair on either edge, pass the weft yarn over the warp and over and around the weft yarn that is behind the warps. You will have twisted the top weft yarn over the bottom weft yarn once between the first and second warp pairs.

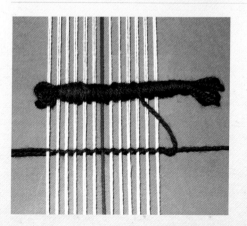

Continue to pass the weft over the next warp pair and around the stationary weft yarn behind the warps until you have twisted the two weft yarns together between all the warp pairs. Be careful not to pull too tightly on the weft as you twine to avoid distorting the warp spacing. When you are finished you should have a single line of weft that wraps in and out of the warps with a twist in between each warp pair.

Weaving the Sheath

Beginning at the right warp edge pick up the first and then every other warp (odd-numbered) with your batten creating the first shed. Using the shuttle card or weft cocoon wrap it once around the stationary weft yarn and place it into the first shed. You can leave the stationary weft end tied to the loom until you have finished weaving.

Pick up the second shed beginning with the second warp and then every other warp (even-numbered). Weave the second shed.

Continue weaving in alternating sheds on all 13 warps for ½ inch. End with your shuttle card or weft cocoon at the right side of the weaving.

To make two slits to attach the sheath to your belt the next ½ inch will be woven as follows: In the next shed weave only the first 4 warps. Continue to weave just these 4 warps back and forth in alternating sheds until the section measures ½ inch. End with the shuttle card or weft cocoon on the right hand side.

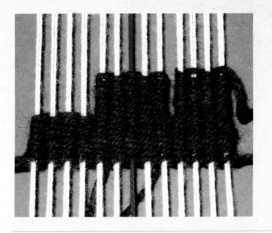

Take a small piece of weft yarn (about 30 inches) and weave the next 5 warps by themselves as you did for the first 4 warps. Weave until this section measures ½ inch to equal the first 4 warps section, ending with the weft yarn on the right side. Leave this weft end to the back of the weaving to be worked in later.

Taking another small piece of weft yarn weave the last 4 warps by themselves as above for ½ inch. Again, ending on the right, leave this weft end to work in later.

Now take the weft on the right edge of the weaving and in the next shed weave all the way across all 12 warps. If the shed does not work with the other woven sections, that is, if it doesn't alternate over and under consistently, you may need to weave an additional row in that section to make the shed work. Continue weaving all 12 warps for another inch.

Your weaving will be about 2 inches long with two ½-inch slits for the belt to go through.

Shaping the Sheath

To shape the sheath you will be decreasing the number of warp yarns that you are weaving on, leaving the outer warps unwoven to create a triangle shape for the sheath.

In the next shed come in one warp on each side (i.e., do not include the first and last warp in this shed). Weave on the inner 11 warp yarns until this section measures one inch.

In the next shed omit one more outer edge warp (i.e., the two outer warps on each side will not be included in this shed). Weave on the inner 9 warp yarns until this section measures one inch.

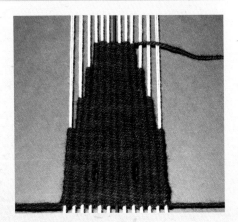

Once again in the next shed omit one more outer edge warp (i.e., there are now four warps on each edge that are not included in the shed). Weave on the inner 5 warp yarns until this section measures one inch.

This completes one side of your sheath.

The Other Side of the Sheath

To make the other side of the sheath you will be reversing the shaping that you did for the first side by increasing the number of warp yarns that you are weaving on.

Continue to weave on the inner 5 warp yarns for another inch. (This section of 4 woven warps will be 2 inches long so when it is folded it will make up the front and back tip of the sheath.)

In the next shed add one warp yarn on each side to the shed. Weave on the inner 7 warp yarns until this section measures one inch.

In the next shed add one warp yarn on each side to the shed. Weave on the inner 9 warp yarns until this section measures one inch.

In the next shed add one warp yarn on each side to the shed. Weave on the inner 11 warp yarns until this section measures one inch.

In the next shed add the last warp yarns on each side to the shed. Weave on all 13 warp yarns until this section measures one inch.

This completes the weaving for the sheath. If you want the front edge of the sheath to be firmer, you can twine this edge the same as you did for the starting edge.

Finishing the Sheath

To remove the sheath from the loom begin by untying the warp yarns from the bottom warp stick of the loom. Tie two adjacent warp ends together in an overhand knot. In the middle, tie one red warp with its adjacent neighbors and the other red warp with its neighboring warps. This will give you a total of 6 knots. Snug these knots as close to the weaving as possible.

Next, carefully cut the warp ends off the top warp stick of the loom. Fold the woven sheath in half lining up the edge. Gently pull on the first two edge warp yarns until the two edges come together and the warp disappears inside the weaving. Tie these two warp ends in an overhand knot close to the weaving.

Repeat with the two outer warp ends on the other side. Take the next two warp ends on each side and pull them into the weaving and tie in an overhand knot close to the weaving. Tie the remaining warp ends close to the weaving. When you have finished you should have a triangular sheath that is connected at 4 points along the sides.

To finish your sheath sew it together along the side edges and work in all the ends with a needle.

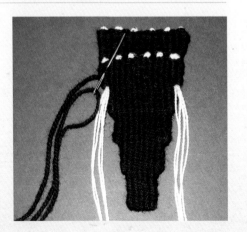

Making the Belt

The belt is made by a simple traditional method of twisting called "twiddling." To make a belt 4½ feet long, you will need to cut 5 pieces of yarn that are 12 feet long. It is easiest to twist the belt with a friend, but you can also do it by yourself by tying one end to a doorknob or chair.

Begin by tying the 5 yarn pieces together with an overhand knot on each end. Next, stretch the yarn out between you and your friend (each one taking an end), or you and the door knob. Facing each other (or facing the door knob) start twisting the yarn bundle in opposite directions (both of you will be twisting to the right), or if by yourself, twist only to the right.

Keep twisting until the yarn bundle tightens and will twist back on itself if you release the tension on the cord between you and your friend (or door knob).

When there is enough twist in the cord, bring the two ends together and hold them while allowing the cord to twist together. Run your hand down the length of the cord several times to smooth out the twist. You should now have a double twisted cord with a loop on one end where it was folded in half and two loose ends.

The Belt of Power

To attach your belt and sheath lace the belt through the slits in the sheath. You can secure your belt around your waist by simply slipping the knotted ends through the loop.

Beads and embroidery can be added to the sheath for adornment. The ends of the belt can be finished with beads or a tassel.

CHAPTER 10

THE MASK: IDENTITY

"Show me your face before you were born."

— Zen koan

The mask which I have come to call the Zati mask came to me in a dream on August 13, 1989. In the dream, I was living near Barcelona, Spain, attending a university. I was to take an exam with lots of other people outside. Tables were set up on a green lawn with the pages of empty blue books fluttering in the breeze. It was hot. The instructor pointed to the tables. I walked straight toward them and then kept going past them down a long slope and out into a wide open field that seemed to glisten with wildflowers and grasses and great oaks beyond. Wandering out into the field, I forgot all about the exam and felt my heart open to the excitement of exploration. Into the hardwoods I went, the sun shining through onto the forest floor.

Before long, I came to an old woods road, where a single bullock cart with large handmade wooden wheels stood unhitched and filled with extraordinary woven masks. I had never seen anything like them before. Each one was like a jewel, woven and felted and embellished with its own headdress. I was curious to see how they were made.

At that moment I saw a group of women on the far side of the wagon wearing long red skirts with aprons. One came to me with a mask in her hands. "This one is for you," she said. She invited me to come and share food with them. I asked, "How do you make these?" And the woman who had given me the mask explained in detail how she had woven mine. She said, "This mask will teach you something very important about yourself. When you find out what that is, share it with others."

That was the gift of the mask.

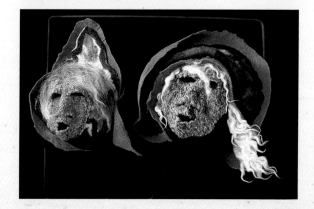

I am a weaver by nature, and at the end of a long rug warp, I tried making what I had seen instructed in the dream. To my surprise, an extraordinary form emerged. Years later, I am still weaving what I have called Zati masks because they arrived and are created from the inside out, bringing into being forgotten aspects of myself.

The Haudenosaunee (Iroquois) Society of Husk Faces or Bushy Heads make masks with corn husks in basketry techniques that are twined, braided, or coiled.[1] Central Africans of Zaire and Congo use woven plant fibers to construct masks.[2] Masks have been made from parts woven with various techniques and assembled together, but to date, I have not found any group of people, historic or current who have woven masks flat on the loom and transformed them three-dimensionally off the loom through weft-wedging techniques. To the best of my knowledge, the masks inspired by the gift of the Spanish woman in the dream are unique in world mask culture.

I wove the Zati masks for over ten years, exploring and wondering. But it wasn't until later that I really started to understand why I was making the masks and what they meant. In our culture, we have completely forgotten the meaning of the mask. It has been suppressed and trivialized because it is so powerful.

As a keyform, the mask is an energetic healing tool. Each one is created for a specific purpose. A mask is the reflection of a soulful condition expressed symbolically to bring it into physical being. It holds the vision still so that you and others can experience it over a period of time. As a healing tool, it is homeopathic in nature (like curing like).

Haudenosaunee shamanic practice with masks heals sickness through mimesis, speaking directly to the spirit of the illness.

The Latin *persona* means "mask." Historically, masks played the role of shifting our point of view from logical to symbolic thinking. Masks act as gatekeepers for the opening between the world of objects and the mystery.

Anyone who has donned a mask and thought about the experience realizes that the mask, in concealing the face, which is the prime expression of the personality, frees something inside. The mask allows us to express other parts of ourselves with a feeling of freedom from our ordinary existence.

So in concealing, the mask paradoxically reveals. The use of masks in evoking spiritual presence is proof of the process. Both the mask-wearer and the viewers of the ritual participate in this joining of their inner selves with a spiritual presence.

Masks reveal the many disguises of their creator's spirit just as our own faces do. Myths and stories begin with concrete experience and evolve into cultural symbols which connect our human lives with the life of the spirit we all recognize. Symbols are able to convey a deeper meaning than literal stories. The mask, when approached with respect for ourselves, can show us our inherent powers of vision and the greater patterns of meaning in our lives.

The spirit of the mask represents a concentration of one's own psychic energy, offering a dialogue between the ego and other aspects of our persona. The mask you make yourself contains power for you because it manifests in concrete form some part of yourself that would like to speak to you. A series of your own masks can reveal to you an entire personal mythology.

Making a mask initiates us into the possibility of identifying with the enlivening force just behind the face we wear every day. The Navaho coming-of-age ceremony for young men involves masks. The moment the Navaho youth looks through the eyes of God in the mask, he becomes a man.

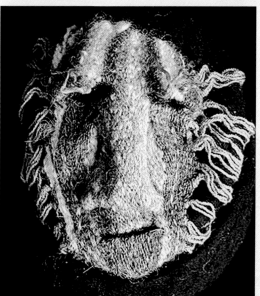

The experience of the mask can be an experience of profound transformation, not as a flash of light, but as an awareness that reverberates inside long after, bringing a slow movement toward your new life. This is how the mask represents a coming of age on your journey.

When you don your mask, you manifest a different portion of your identity. Moreover, you animate the inanimate material of the mask. Roberta and Peter Markman, in *Masks of the Spirit,* describe this relationship:

> "On the one hand, the mask is a lifeless, material thing animated by the wearer, exactly, of course, the relationship between human beings and the gods: human beings are created from lifeless matter by the animating force of the divine, and life exists only as long as it is supported by that divine force. Thus the wearer of the mask almost literally becomes the god; he is, for the moment the animating force within the otherwise lifeless mask. But at the same time, the mask expresses outwardly, the inner spiritual identity of the wearer, that is the life force within the microcosm and is thus a truer reflection of the wearer's spiritual essence than his so-called real, or natural face."[3]

Thus, masks have the potential of becoming teachers of the nature of creation itself. Identity and the power of personal choice have been at the heart of my work for over thirty-five years as a weaver, teacher, career counselor, and life coach. But it wasn't until I was given the gift of the Zati woven mask in a dream that I was able to make the connection between the art of weaving and the art of living. Making choices that give me the power to love my life has been the key to my personal transformation.

The mask is not a plaything, nor is it an idol to worship. It embodies and evokes a revelation of unseen parts of ourselves. Care and reverence in the crafting and wearing of the mask deepen our awareness and create an atmosphere for the integration of the personae that initiate identification with our soul.

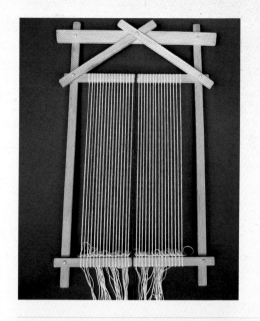

INSTRUCTIONS:
The Secret of Weaving the Zati Mask

Warping the Loom

To make the mask begin with 33 warp yarns that are 54 inches long. Tie these 33 warp yarns onto the loom with the tie at the bottom warp stick (See pages 22–24 for directions on warping the loom). Space the warp yarns ¼ inch apart (4 ends per inch). Your warp will be approximately eight inches wide.

The mask is woven sideways on the loom with the chin on one side and the forehead on the other. The warp thus runs across the face instead of from forehead to chin. The face created with eight shapes on each side. In practice, these are often blended together, with the unwoven warp spaces allowing for shaping of the mask. Once the mask is woven it is taken off the loom and the warp yarns are pulled to shape the mask.

The Right Side of the Face

Beginning at the right warp edge, pick up every other warp yarn creating your first shed. Place the weft cocoon through this shed weaving all the warp yarns. Next, pick up the opposite warp yarns from the first shed (creating the second shed), and weave all the warp yarns with the weft yarn. You will now have two rows of weaving in two alternate sheds. You may weave up to an inch here, depending on how wide you want the face.

Pick up the next shed warps from the outer edge to the middle red centering warp. Weave just the first half of the warps in this shed ending with your weft cocoon at the red center warp.

Beginning at the red center warp you will now be weaving in alternating sheds, adding one more warp yarn on each outer edge in each shed as you go. You will be creating a "V" shape that expands from the center to the outer edges one warp yarn each row until your last row, when all warps have been woven. End with your weft cocoon at the left edge.

The Right Eyebrow and Eye

In the next shed, working left to right, pick up and weave on only the first 10 warps (6 warps from the red center warp). Weave in alternating sheds on these 10 warps only for 1½ inches to create the right eye.

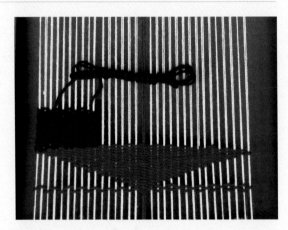

The Right Cheek and Eye

With a new weft cocoon, at the bottom edge of the square you just wove, pick up and weave the remaining 23 unwoven warps only. Continue weaving in alternating sheds on these 23 warps for approximately ¾ inch (or to the center of the eye). End with your weft cocoon at the left (eye) edge.

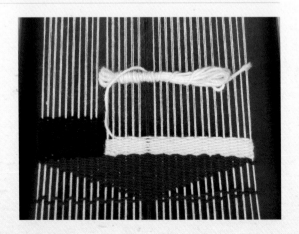

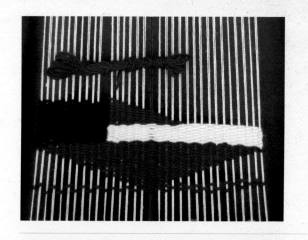

The relationship of the eye and nose: the right nostril starts at the mid-eye and ends at the inner edge of the eye. Begin the eye: in the next shed pick up and weave the next 11 warps (4 warps beyond the red center warp). You will be creating the first triangular shape that will be the under eye/cheek to the right of the nose. Continue to weave on only these 11 warp yarns, omitting one warp on the right side edge in each shed until you have only one warp woven on the eye edge.

This completes the first eye.

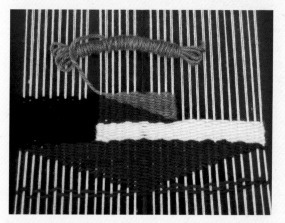

The Right Side of the Nose

With a new weft cocoon beginning at the nostril edge (the point of the triangle just woven, 4 warps to the right of the red center warp), pick up and weave one warp. In each alternating shed continue to pick up one more warp on the left side in each shed until you have woven on all 11 warps and created a mirror image triangle to the one you just wove.

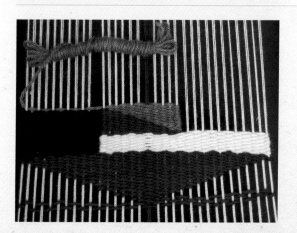

After you have completed the right nose triangle, pick up and weave the remaining warps above the eye (10 warps) with the nostril weft cocoon. If the shed does not work to continue above the eye, weave one more row above the eye with the eyebrow weft cocoon, and then continue with the nose weft cocoon in the shed, ending with the weft cocoon at the left edge.

The Upper Lip

With a new weft cocoon, pick up and weave in alternating sheds the 4 warp yarns to the right of the nose edge. Begin at the nose edge and weave back and forth on only these 4 warps until equal in length with the right half of the nose.

Now, with the nose weft cocoon pick up and weave the 10 brow warps, the 11 nose warps, and the 4 upper lip warps creating the middle of the brow, the nose ridge, and the middle of the upper lip. Weave 2 to 3 more rows on these 25 warps from the brow edge to the upper lip edge. End with your weft cocoon at the left brow edge.

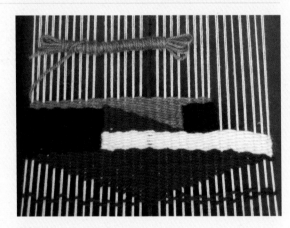

The Mouth and Chin

With a new weft cocoon or shuttle card, beginning at the lip edge, pick up one warp and weave. Continue weaving in alternating sheds adding one warp in each shed on the right side as you go until all 8 warps have been woven. Weave on all 8 warps for 3 rows. This completes the first half of your mask.

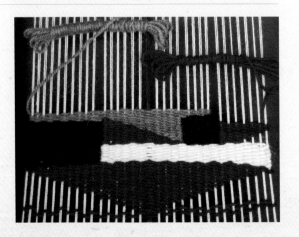

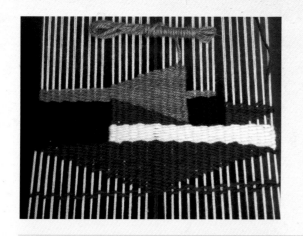

The Left Side of the Nose

With the nose weft cocoon or shuttle card pick up and weave the warps from the brow (10 warps) and the nose (11 warps), 4 warps to the right of the red center warp. Weave 2 rows on these warps only. Now pick up and weave to 6 rows to the left of the red center warp for the second eye. Weave in alternating sheds on these 11 warps, creating a triangle by omitting one warp on the left edge in each row until only one warp remains at the nose edge.

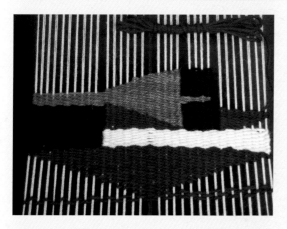

The Left Upper Lip

With a new weft cocoon or shuttle card, pick up and weave the 4 warp yarns of the upper lip. Weave on only these 4 warps until the upper lip measures the same as the nose.

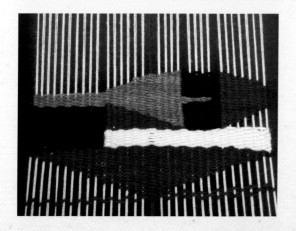

The Chin

With the chin cocoon or shuttle card, pick up and weave in alternating sheds 5 rows. In the next shed beginning at the right edge, omit one warp in each shed as you weave until you have only one warp remaining at the mouth edge. There will be unwoven warps on either side of the chin which will be used to create the shaping when you are done weaving.

The Left Cheek and Eye

With a new weft cocoon or shuttle card, beginning at the eye edge, pick up one warp and weave. Continue to weave in alternating sheds, adding one warp to the right edge in each shed as you go, until all 11 warps have been woven. This is the mirror image triangle for the left half of the nose.

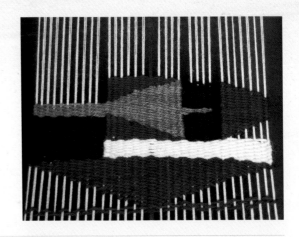

The Left Brow

With a new weft cocoon or shuttle card, pick up and weave the 10 warps for the left brow. Weave in alternating sheds on these 10 warps until the brow measures 1½ inches.

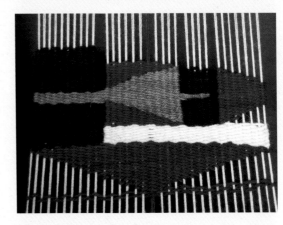

The Left Cheek

With a new weft cocoon or shuttle card, pick up and weave the remaining 23 unwoven warps for approximately ¾ inch to match the right cheek. If the first shed does not match up, weave one more row where needed (i.e., in the left cheek/under eye, upper lip, or chin piece) to make a complete shed in these 23 warps.

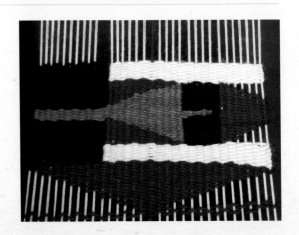

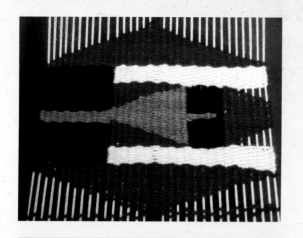

With a new weft cocoon or shuttle card, pick up and weave all 33 warps. Continue to weave in alternating sheds, omitting one warp on both outer edges in each shed as you go, until only the red center warp remains.

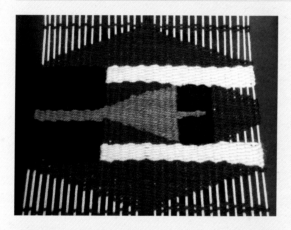

In the next shed, weave all the way to the outer edge. Weave at least two more rows on all 33 warps. You may add up to an inch here to fill out the width of the face. This completes the weaving of your mask.

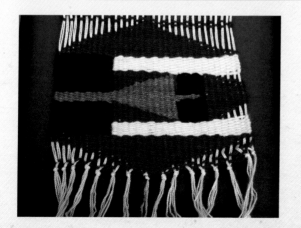

Removing the Mask from the Loom

Take a moment and consider what is about to take place.

To remove the mask from the loom, untie the warp yarns from the bottom warp stick and tie them together two at a time next to the weaving. (Tie one of the red warp yarns with its neighboring warps, and the other red warp yarn with its neighboring warps.) Cut the other ends of the warps from the top warp stick of the loom. Do not tie them yet.

Shaping the Mask

This is where the character of your mask will reveal itself. Beginning with the center warp yarns, gently pull the warps to shape the mask. Work from the inner warps to the outer warps gently tightening as you go. The lower eye warp can be pulled slightly tighter than the upper eye warp to shape the eyes.

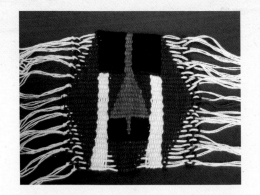

To shape the nose, pull tighter on the lower nose warp and insert your fingers into the nostril as you tighten the upper nostril warp, creating an opening for the nostril. Repeat for the mouth. Work with your mask, molding it with your fingers as you pull on the warp yarns. Pay close attention to what the face is doing: don't force it, but let the mask take its own shape. Each one will be different, and each will surprise you. When you have found your mask, tie the remaining untied warp ends together. Your mask is now ready for adornment.

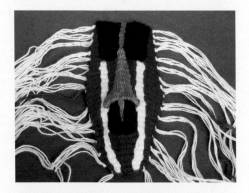

CHAPTER 11

THE BUNDLE: TAKING HOLD

"Not I—not anyone else, can travel that road for you.
You must travel it for yourself."

— Walt Whitman

In the tradition of Chinese medicine there is an ancient configuration in which all that exists has a place on the wheel of transformation. Sequential and simultaneous, the circle works in parts or as a whole. Water Energy at the base of the wheel is floating like water in the night, or the stillness of winter. Tree or Wood Energy to the left of the wheel flows upward like the morning sun and spring with sap rising. Fire Energy is placed at the top of the wheel and expands outward like noon and the heat of the summer sun. Soil Energy placed in the upper right of the wheel is downward, associated with afternoon energy and those golden late summer days. Metal Energy is low on the right of the wheel and represents a gathering in, evening and late autumn.[1] This is the Energy of the Bundle, a drawing inward to examine what we have collected and once again to decide what is valuable, what is sacred.

The bundle is similar to the amulet, but fundamentally different. The amulet calls in our power at the beginning of our quest; the bundle is the toolkit of the inner journey.

The Zati bundle is a woven bag a little bigger than your hand, that can attach to your belt of power, be worn around the neck, or kept in an honored place. It is made for collecting small objects that are significant only to you, with the purpose of practicing how to hold as sacred what you love. Metaphorically, it is made for collecting all the energy of your attention. As we move through our day, our mind goes out on to everything it sees and hears and smells and tastes and touches like sticky fingers attaching themselves to whatever they notice. We become so expanded that we are mentally touching people and events all over the world. We pick up every airwave in our mental radius, like a radio antenna, alive with the fears and worries of millions.

Once you have entered the turning point, seen into the mystery, and recognized your true identity through the mask, the bundle is the keyform you use while walking the rest of the way home.

Thread by thread we begin to detach our attention from the noises of the world and bring our attention, our awareness, into our bundle. Developmentally, the keyform of the bundle is a coming of age between your fifties and seventies, although in every day we have this time in the late afternoon or before going to bed. This is the time to practice sorting the seeds that belong to you. What is really worthy of your time and attention? Emblems of these are what make your bundle sacred. What you devote your talent, resources, time, and attention to make up the colors, textures, and patterns of your life. The beauty you are looking for in your weaving can only come with an awareness of the threads you are carrying across the threshold of your life, lacing through the warp of your innermost beliefs and beating into the weft of your days.

Every evening, bring back home all of the attention you have spread out during the day, every last object of it. Look at your collection daily and decide what you want to keep in your bundle. Your awareness creates who you are. When that belongs to you instead of to everyone else, you have the freedom to weave the life you choose.

Whatever is valuable enough to keep in your bundle is then sacred to you. The bundle is what belongs to you. Only you are allowed to open your own bundle. Only you know what you have put in it and what the contents mean to you. Just as you do not know how it feels to live in someone else's body, no one knows how you are in your own skin. This separation does not alienate us from the world, but allows us to come to it in our full power, on our terms.

Our bodies are also our sacred bundles. We enliven what we consider sacred with the intensity of our attention. Even if the bundle and all its contents are not perceived by anyone else to be valuable, it is a container which exists as witness to your unique experience. First you have to know how to hold yourself in order ultimately to let go. In order to unite with the One within, we have to lose our belief in our separate identity. Paradoxically, if we don't know who we are in the mental and social sense, this loss is impossible: you can't lose what you don't have. You have to develop the ego in a healthy way in order to dissociate from it inside. The ultimate goal of every spiritual master and every path is the loss of the illusion of individuality, and the attainment of the awareness of unity with all. Ultimately our bundle will be empty, for we will have nothing to contain. We see ourselves as a drop of water in a bottle floating in the ocean of life. When we allow the bottle to disappear, the drop becomes the whole ocean.

Until then, we have a tendency to want to give ourselves away. Why is that? One reason is that we all want to be loved; when we find we have something everyone wants, without understanding, we start handing it out. After all, we are taught to share! But when we do that indiscriminately, we discover that what we had is quickly dissipating. What we have inside is our own experience; no one else can have that experience.

Another reason we share our inner experiences is that it makes us feel superior. I have spiritual experiences, and I want everyone to know so they will think I am a wise being. Ego can trick us into giving away the treasure we have. The treasure dissolves when we don't value it. We have to learn how to become a vessel and to contain our own power. We grow into our greater self slowly as we are able.

In the sacred bundle I weave are the things that are just for me in my life. I do not share them with anyone. I practice keeping them for myself, because I must travel the road myself. I do not reveal the contents of my bundle to anyone: it is my secret. It took me many years to attain a bundle just for myself. I had always thought it was selfish, that I should not hide or hold anything. What I have come to realize is that if I allow myself to have things that are sacred only to me, I know what I really value. The hard-won awareness we gain cannot be transferred to anyone else; no one else can value it, because they have not worked to gain it. I remember that what I am inside will reveal itself outside: the bowl and the doll showed me that the outer shape is determined by what is inside. My life is more valuable to others when I value it more myself.

When wisdom has been given to me, how can I learn the art of holding that power? As I grow the sacred space within myself it begins to emanate into my environment, and I become aware of myself within the bundle of this earth.

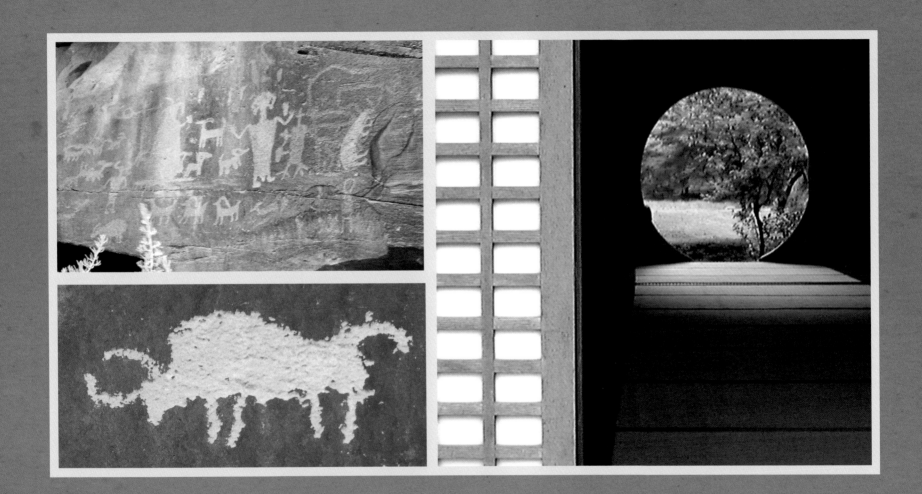

INSTRUCTIONS: *The Bundle*

Warping the Loom

To make your bundle begin with 31 warp yarns that are 54 inches long. Tie these 31 warp yarns onto the loom with the tie at the bottom warp stick of the loom. (See pages 22–24 for directions on warping the loom.) Space the warp yarns ¼ inch apart or 4 ends per inch. Your warp will be about 7 inches wide.

Weaving the Bundle

Like the mask, the bundle is woven sideways on the loom such that the width of the weaving is the length of the bundle. This bundle will be woven with three weft colors. For your first shed, beginning at the left warp edge, pick up and weave every other warp with your first weft color cocoon or shuttle card. Leave a two-inch tail at the left edge.

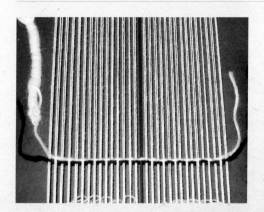

To create the second shed pick up the opposite warp yarns from the first shed. Weave this shed using your second weft color shuttle card or cocoon, going from right to left and leaving a two-inch tail at the right edge.

The third shed is the same as the first shed, but is woven with the third weft color from left to right, leaving a two inch tail at the left edge. While this shed is open, take the two-inch tail from weft color number one, and weave it into this shed an inch or so. Bring the end to the back of your weaving to anchor it.

Continue to weave in alternating sheds using these three weft colors. At the end of each row you will have two weft colors on one side, and one weft color on the other side. Your next weft color to use will always be the weft color under the one you just finished using. Simply wrap the new weft color around the weft you just finished with, and place it in the next shed. This technique will give you a nice finished edge for the top and bottom of your bundle.

Continue to weave in this manner until the woven piece measures 10 inches long.

Removing the Bundle from the Loom

Untie the warp yarns from the bottom warp stick of the loom. Next, cut the warp ends from the top warp stick of the loom.

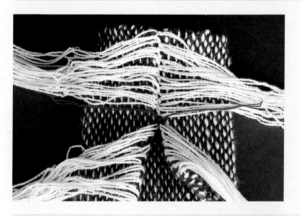

Finishing the Bundle

Fold the woven piece to form a tube with the warp ends together. Tie the warp ends together end to end next to the weaving, creating the center seam of your bundle.

With the warp ends seam at the center of your bundle, use a piece of weft yarn and sew along the bottom selvege edge of the bundle.

The warp ends can be adorned with beads for decoration or worked back into the weaving to finish.

Making the Bundle Cord

To make a cord for the bundle handle/tie you can make a twisted cord (see instructions at the end of the Belt of Power) or a simple braided cord from your left over weft yarn.

Attaching the Cord to the Bundle

Beginning at the center back of the bundle take one end of the cord and lace it through the weaving about ¼ inch down from the top edge to the center of the front. Repeat with the other half of the cord for the other half of the bundle, having both ends come out together in the center front of the bundle. Tie these two ends together in an overhand knot or add a large bead. This knot or bead will allow you to draw the cord tight and cinch the bundle closed by simply pulling on the cord at the back of the bundle.

CHAPTER 12

THE SHAWL:
LIVING THE INNER LIFE

"Thoroughly to know oneself is above all art,
for it is the highest art."

— Theologica Germanics

The shawl is that ancient and simple piece of cloth that humans use to cover themselves, forming a sculpture around the shoulders and head, in many forms and materials, across all the continents and seas of the world. From times before history to this moment, the shawl has given warmth when it's cold, protection from rain and wind and sun. The shawl protects and encloses: it forms one's own private space. When you have followed the thread of the keyforms to the shawl, their combined meaning will take a larger shape. Each keyform is a piece of a puzzle that becomes whole as your awareness of the bigger picture grows. If we want to transform ourselves, we have to become aware of how we are greater than we have previously imagined.

The loom creates a framework for our point of view; the warp, a ground for our intentions, woven into our daily actions. Intention determines the shape of all our future forms. The shawl is made of ten different rectangular weavings, woven with one intention. It is different from the other keyforms in two ways.

First of all, it cannot be woven all at once. It takes time and perseverance. One shape 10 different times, this is the practice. No two will be the same and yet they will all fit together to create a whole fabric. This is the work of persisting in your purpose. The second difference is that the shape of the shawl is not built into it, but forms itself around you. In the final keyform, You are the form.

Practicing love for yourself is the primary objective of Weaving a Life. All other attributes and abilities to love others are connected to this practice. Centering, gratitude, and forgiveness are the benefits you will receive when you practice them as you weave in and out of the warp. First you call in your intentions as you make the amulet. Then you are able to view your work as a gift of love to yourself, and with the creation of the bowl you are able to receive love. By owning this gift to yourself, you become strong and begin nurturing yourself as you create the doll, a way to envision your wisdom self. Then the core work of standing up to the negative downward energies that keep you from experiencing the love that is always around and within you begin with the belt of power and your knife of discrimination. The mask is the quest for identity, the quest to experience the truth of yourself. The bundle gathers all your attention into a place of safety and peace and the shawl gives you time and comfort and a quiet space to practice until you have woven the life you imagined. Then, you yourself become the gift for others.

The shawl has been associated with meditation since the beginning of time. When one has no separate room or privacy, the shawl creates a sacred space. As we wrap ourselves day after day in our meditation, we associate the shawl with the peace inside. The shawl is the universal piece of cloth to wrap around your shoulders and embrace your own heart with love. When you are weary from doing the work it takes just to be in this world, to make a living and raise a family and care for those who cared for you, you can wrap yourself in the folds of the shawl, and find yourself wrapped in folds of peace.

The shawl is your final keyform. Developmentally, it is the time of ripening, the time of harvest. Coming of age in this time is to allow your weaving to surround and support you. It is time to let go. Let go, let go—we've heard this a thousand times. What exactly will we let go? At the beginning of this journey of weaving your life, you receive your whole self as a separate entity by weaving the receiving bowl, complete and beautiful. Now, like water flowing into the sea, you can let go of the self as a separate being. You can sink the bowl in the sea of yourself, and become the whole ocean which is the divine Self.

Originally, when working out the ideas that have come to life in this book, I saw the shawl as a shroud. It is natural to fear death, and it is the work of developing consciousness to confront that fear with love. Spiritual teachers say the union with the One is like death. It is not bodily death, but is a temporary death of individuality, of personality, of separateness. If the shawl is the shroud of the ego, it is also the receiving blanket of newborn love.

"'Tis only the semblance of death—in reality it is a migration."

— Rumi

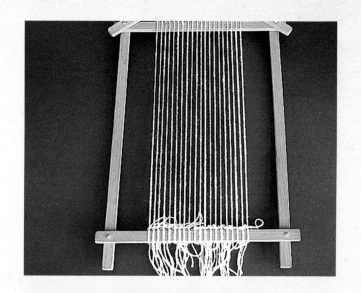

INSTRUCTIONS: *The Shawl*

Warping the Loom

To create your shawl, you will be making 10 rectangular woven pieces that will be sewn together. The instructions for the woven panels are the same for all 10 pieces but you may choose to weave different colors and patterns into each of your 10 pieces. To make a woven panel begin with 21 warp yarns that are 54 inches long (except for the last panel which will require 42 warp yarns that are 36 inches long). Tie these 21 warp yarns onto the loom (see pages 22–24 for directions on warping the loom). Space the warp yarns ¼ inch apart (4 threads per inch). Your finished panel will measure approximately 8 inches wide by 13 inches long.

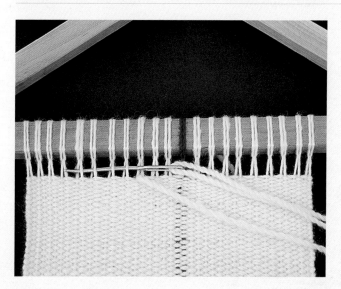

Weaving the Shawl

Begin weaving at the very bottom of the loom. In this weaving you will be using each individual warp yarn separately (instead of in pairs as in the other keyforms) so you will be weaving on 42 warps. This allows for a finer weave. You will want to weave fairly loosely (do not pack the weft too tight) to create a soft fabric for your shawl.

Continue weaving on all 42 warps until you have filled the entire warp (approximately 13 inches long). As you get closer to the top of the weaving it may become difficult to pass the weft cocoon through the shed. Use a tapestry needle to weave the last few inches.

Removing the Woven Panel from the Loom

Untie the warp yarns from the bottom stick of the loom. Tie two adjoining warp ends together with an overhand knot. You will need to tie one of the red center warp yarns with two adjoining warp ends and the other red center warp yarn with its neighboring warp yarns.

To remove the panel from the top stick of the loom unscrew the wing nuts holding the stick to the loom, remove the screw on one side, and slide the warp ends off the stick. Do not cut these warp ends, you will need the loops to attach the panel ends together.

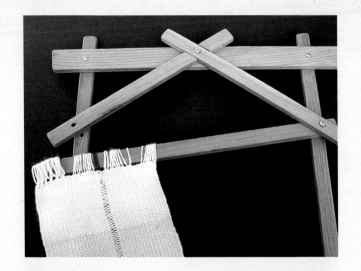

Warping and Weaving the Last Panel

Warping the last panel for the shawl is a little different from the other 9 panels. For the last panel you will need 42 warp yarns that are 36 inches long. To warp this panel take two warp yarns and tie an overhand knot 6 inches from the ends. Place this knot on the top warp stick and bring one end to the front and one end to the back of the loom. Keeping these two warp yarns parallel tie them at the bottom stick the same way you tied the warps for the previous panels. This panel is warped in this manner so when you are finished weaving the piece you will have enough warp remaining on each end of the panel for a 6 inch fringe. Weave this panel as you did the other 9 panels.

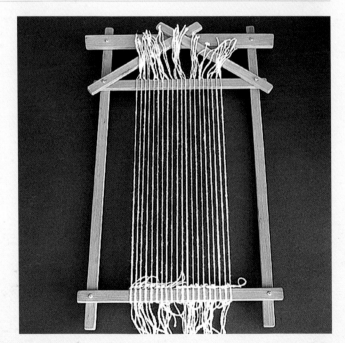

To remove this panel from the loom, untie the warps at the bottom and tie two together in an overhand knot as you did for the other panels.

Untie the knots at the top warp stick of the loom, and retie them close to the weaving in overhand knots, as you did for the other end.

Sewing the Shawl

The shawl is created by attaching the panels together end to end in four rows. The first row will consist of 4 panels attached together. The second row will consist of 3 panels attached together. The third row consists of 2 panels and the last row is the last panel you wove which has the fringe on both ends. For the first row, lay out the four panels you will be using, making sure that the two outer panels have fringe ends on the outside. Tie the warp ends of the adjoining panels together. Lay out and tie the warp ends together for the second and third rows.

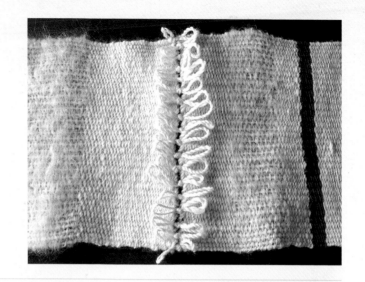

Sew the rows together as follows: Sew the first row (4 panels) to the second row (3 panels) by starting the outside edge of the second row at the midpoint of the first panel on the first row and ending at the midpoint of the last panel of the first row. Sew the third row (2 panels) to the second row (3 panels) in the same manner. Sew the last panel to the third row, centering it in the middle of the two panels of the third row. Trim all the outside fringe to 6 inches. You may choose to adorn your shawl, for example by tying beads to the fringe or adding fringe to the bottom of the last row.

CHAPTER 13

THE GIFT: LEGACY OF LOVE

"The great teachers who proclaim the truth
use varying forms to put it in,
yet the truth contained in all is one."

— Upanishads

The great gift in Weaving a Life is that we can learn to see all of life as one weaving. We are woven together by invisible threads, part of the web of the universe. Breathing in and out, who we are, does make a difference to all life. We arc either contributing to the general confusion and chaos of the world by living a fragmented life, or tuned to the energy that unifies, weaving our mind, body, and spirit into a spacious awareness of ourselves as Love. There is no concept of good or bad here, only an awareness of what takes us closer to our source and what leads us further from it.

Through our surrender to love, we find the power we have been seeking all along. The paradox of surrender as the path to power is based on giving up our need to control others. By choosing love, we create peace. That is our legacy. Love is the essential material of which all creation is made. When we tune into and work with that higher vibration already within us, we tune into the essence of the Creator, the source of Love.

Each of these projects is a practice to establish a more loving relationship with yourself. Through the process of weaving all seven keyforms, you have completed a circle, bringing you around the heart of yourself through your hands. You are balanced and grounded in your center. You discover that the choices that nurture you in turn nurture others.

The Gift of the Journey

I have created a simple and beautiful space for all of my keyforms with a place for me to sit and contemplate my journey. I pick a time of day when I will not be interrupted and allow myself to become aware of any issues or obstacles that are keeping me from feeling love. Now that I am aware of my responsibility to choose my response, I understand the opportunity I have to be intentional rather than react. I wrap my shawl around me and close my eyes. There I am with myself. If I can shed the distractions of the day and collect myself at my center, I am with my own true self.

In my imagination, I put the issue in front of me and look at it through the view finder of my loom. What is my point of view? Where am I coming from? Where am I looking? Is there an obstacle that stands in my way?

Next I warp my loom, first centering myself with the red thread and coming to my heart. It is a practiced center. The more we use any of the keyforms, the more we will hear the song that is ours alone, and learn how to sing it. That is where the power comes from and that is the key to personal power, learning to sing your inherent song, the song that is a note of the inner melody, a thread of the universal warp.

Now comes the process of retracing the steps of the journey.

Take a deep breath and center yourself. Go to your heart. Plant the seed of love and watch it grow. Sit with your heart radiating love to every cell in your body, to the space around you, to the world and the universe. Love whatever comes before you in your field of inner vision. Come back to your body in your heart and see what needs your attention. Sit with whatever energy appears to need your attention and surround it with love. Get bigger than the small energy. Receive yourself wholeheartedly just the way you are in the present moment with gratitude. Then protect your love with the knowledge that there is nothing more powerful on earth than love: hold only love. You are ready to journey through the memory of each keyform.

Recall your intention, which is woven into your amulet. This prepared you for the journey you have taken. What is your intention now? Where is your journey taking you?

As the bowl has an outside and an inside, leave everything else outside, and hold only love inside. You shape yourself to the container and the container shapes itself to you. What shape is your love?

Bring your doll into your inner vision. Allow her to sit quietly with you. What wisdom can you discover with her today? If she were your wise woman in the woods, as in the story, what would your conversation be?

With your inner vision wrap your belt of power around your waist. How will you enclose your sacred space? Tell all inner messages that want to take you away from your wisdom and love that they may now leave or be transformed into harmonies that will help you today.

Know that as the day progresses you are willing, with the will of a warrior, to dissolve and transform what keeps you in a knot in order to create an atmosphere of light. Hold fast to your belt of power, because your lower mind is going to want to argue you out of your own wisdom. Here you can choose what you want to listen to. When you hear your own truth, you will feel a sense of peace.

When that comes to you, you are ready for your mask to help you identify consistently with this higher point of view, to see yourself with new eyes and to see the world with the eyes of the Creator in you.

Now hold who you are in your own sacred bundle; remember, protect, and bear the tools of the journey of love.

You have prepared yourself and gathered the means for the inner journey. Now wrap yourself in the folds of love.

When you give the gift of love to yourself, you have it to give to others. When you have created peace in your own heart, you bring peace into your community. With the confidence that comes with the power of love, you will transform the lives of everyone you touch.

"I weave the cloth of
the Creator's Name
To remove the twists and twirls
That entangle my being
I remain absorbed in Love.
...
While engaged in such Weaving
I realized my own true self."

— Kabir[1]

EarthLoom in garden project at Troy Howard Middle School, Belfast, Maine

APPENDIX: THE EARTHLOOM

"The first peace, which is the most important, is that which comes within the souls of people when they realize their relationship, their oneness, with the universe and all its powers, and when they realize that at the center of the universe dwells the Great Spirit, and that this center is really everywhere—it is within each of us."

— Black Elk

The experiences you've gained through your Weaving a Life journey can be expanded into your community! The nine-foot EarthLoom is a living symbol, planted in the ground, of our intention to weave together the fabric of community. Just as the Journey Loom is a means for the individual to study integration of the self, the EarthLoom helps communities to unite hands and hearts to build and weave together an emblem and an instrument of peace. With many hands on both sides of the loom, we use our differences to create art in which every contribution is vital to the design as a whole.

Your EarthLoom may be built by your organization, corporation, school, family, camp, day care, hospital, prison, government agency, nursing home, or in your garden or back yard. EarthLooms and their weavings are a gift of friendship and an inspiration for action.

Children and adults can weave together. Some weavers may begin at the top, while others weave from the bottom, until they meet in the middle. People in wheelchairs can come right up to the loom and weave, with room for two on each side.

EarthLooms may be made with indigenous materials by the hands of those who will weave on them. Weaving together is so powerful—it is a literal act of weaving together the community. In this simple and ancient art, we connect with others whose fingers have touched the same threads to create the same fabric with the same purpose. It is a deep-rooted bond in the heart that can change the way we define our neighborhood.

For more information visit www.earthloom.org

NOTES

The following include bibliographic references for information and concepts cited, as well as references for works quoted in the text. All excerpts of works by other authors are used by permission.

Epigraph & Introduction

1. Lekh Raj Puri, *Radha Swami Teachings* (New Delhi: L. R. Puri), 71. Used by permission.

2. Puri, *Radha Swami Teachings,* 71.

3. Puri, *Radha Swami Teachings,* 70.

Chapter 1

1. Elizabeth Wayland Barber, *Women's Work: The First 20,000 Years* (New York: W. W. Norton, 1994), 26.

2. Joseph Campbell, *Hero with a Thousand Faces* (New York: The World Publishing Company, 1971), 217–218. Used by permission of the Joseph Campbell Foundation.

Chapter 3

1. Dario Valcarenghi, *Kilim History and Symbols* (New York: Electa/Abbeville, 1994), 9–10. Used by permission of the author.

2. Brian W. MacDonald, *Tribal Rugs: Treasures of the Black Tent* (New York: Antique Collector's Club, 1997), 23.

3. Valcarenghi, *Kilim History and Symbols,* 9.

Chapter 4

1. Hernan Oliva, conversations with the author, 2002.

2. Hector Esponda Dubin, *Living Meditation* (Punjab, India: Radha Soami Satsang Beas, 2004), 29. Used by permission.

Chapter 5

1. Vacarenghi, *Kilim History and Symbols,* 9.

2. Barber, *Women's Work,* 26.

3. Dubin, *Living Meditation,* 36.

4. Campbell, *Hero with a Thousand Faces,* 25.

Chapter 6

1. Janet Harvey, *Traditional Textiles of Central Asia* (London: Thames and Hudson, 1996), 43.

Chapter 7

1. From "Come Wild Women," poem by Susan Merrill.

2. Andrew Harvey, "On Gratitude," from *Light Upon Light* by Andrew Harvey, 149, © 1996 by Andrew Harvey. Used by permission of Jeremy P. Tarcher, an imprint of Penguin Group (USA) Inc.

Chapter 9

1. Unpublished story by Susan Merrill.

2. Pauline Campanelli, *Wheel of the Year:*

Living the Magical Life (St. Paul, MN: Llewellyn Publishing, 2000), 20.

3. Dubin, *Living Meditation,* 36.

4. Julian Johnson, *The Path of the Masters* (Amritsar, India: Radha Swami Satsang Beas, 1985), 256. Used by permission.

5. Carmine Leo, conversation with the author, January 2005.

Chapter 10

1. William Fenton, *The False Faces of the Iroquois* (Norman, OK: University of Oklahoma Press, 1987).

2. Detroit Institute of Arts, Mwaash a Mbooy, Mukyeem mask, http://www.dia.org.

3. Roberta Markman and Peter Markman, *Masks of the Spirit: Image and Metaphor in Mesoamerica* (Berkeley: University of California Press, 1989), xix–xx. Used by permission.

Chapter 11

1. "Wheel of Five Transformations" as taught at the Kushi Institute, Becket, MA, Macrobiotic Newsletter, April 2002.

Chapter 13

1. V. K. Sethi, *Kabir, the Weaver of God's Name,* trans. V. K. Sethi (Punjab, India: Radha Soami Satsang Beas, 1984), 193. Used by permission.

GLOSSARY

Batten: The flat stick with a slight point at one end used to pick up every other thread of the warp to create a shed, an opening for the yarn to pass through the vertical threads of the weaving. When this stick has been "woven" all the way through the warp, it can be turned on its side to keep the shed open, enabling you to pass the weft (horizontal) yarn all the way across the interior of the weaving. Then the batten may be used as a beater to secure the woven yarn in place.

Cocoon: A tightly wound bundle of yarn used like a shuttle.

Fiber: The raw material that makes the yarns and felt used in weaving and felting. Animal fibers such as wool and mohair and vegetable fibers such as flax and cotton have individual filaments or fibers which are twisted together to make yarn.

Handwoven: Woven by hand.

Keyform: A word created by the author to describe the weavings in this book, which embody elemental forms and experiences common to humans throughout history.

Plain weave: The weave in which the weft alternates going over and under each pair of warp threads

Pulled warp: A technique to make flat weaving sculptural by pulling individual warp threads after the weaving is taken off the loom.

Shed: In hand weaving, the space created between upper and lower threads of the warp after they have been separated by the batten and the batten is turned on its side.

Selvedge: The vertical edges of the fabric, where the weft turns back into the warp for each row, created as you weave.

Shuttle: The carrier for the yarn which is pulled through the shed.

Shuttle card: Small oval card with slits, which holds yarn for hand weaving and tapestry weaving.

Tapestry: A weaving technique in which the weft covers the warp. Patterns are made with many short weft threads instead of a single long one. The term for this is "discontinuous weft threads."

Thread: Fibers twisted together into a strand. See *Yarn*. In weaving, the terms thread and yarn are sometimes used interchangeably. In general, we refer to the warp as thread, and the weft as yarn. Thinner strands are thread; thicker are yarn.

Warp: The group of vertical parallel threads, held under tension on a loom, through which the weft is passed during the weaving process.

Warp pairs: The use of two parallel warp threads as one, usually by doubling one thread as on the Journey Loom.

Weft: The yarn used to weave in and out of the warp threads which creates the woven web.

Weaving: The interlacing of vertical and horizontal threads

Yarn: Fibers twisted together to form a strand. Usually yarn refers to the thicker strands used for knitting and weaving. Thinner strands, such as those used for sewing, may be called threads.

Zati: A word from the Urdu language (northern India and Pakistan) meaning *essential, intrinsic, natural, fundamental*; also translated as *from the inside out,* or *from a sacred place.*

PHOTO CREDITS

Photo credits are listed from top to bottom for each page. All photos are used by permission of photographers.

Cover art and frontispiece photos by Richard Merrill. Acknowledgments photo courtesy of Wednesday Spinners. Title watercolor: *Salt Hay Marsh* by Susan Grabara, 1985.

Introduction

i: Susan Merrill ii: Ken Woisard; iii: Richard Merrill

Chapter 1

1: Susan Merrill; 2: Jani Estell; 3: top, William Thuss; bottom, Susan Merrill; 5: Brad Mering

Chapter 2

6–7: Brian Lary, 8: Paul Kempin; 9: Alexander Shelgunov, 10: Richard Merrill; 11: David Meyer

Chapter 3

12–13: Turkmen girls weaving in Andkhoy, Afghanistan, courtesy Barakat, Inc.; 14 top: Susan Merrill; 14 bottom: Richard Merrill; 15 top: F. Smith; 15 bottom: Susan Merrill; 16–17: illustrations by Richard Merrill

Chapter 4

18–21: Susan Merrill; 22–24: illustrations by Richard Merrill; 25: unknown (antique photo in author's collection)

Chapter 5

26–27: Susan Merrill; 28 top: T. Denham; middle: "tfwww"; bottom: Susan Merrill; 29–31: Susan Merrill; 32–33: Photos and drawings by Richard Merrill

Chapter 6

35: photo of Emily Seger by Susan Merrill; 36–39, 40 top left, bottom left, Susan Merrill; 40 bottom right: Jani Estell, 41: Geri Valentine

Chapter 7

46–47, 48, 49, 51: Susan Merrill; 50: Jani Estell

Chapter 8

58–59, 60 bottom: Jani Estell; 60 top, 61 top & bottom: Susan Merrill; 62, 63: Jani Estell

Chapter 9

70–71, 73: Susan Merrill; 72 top: Werner Braun; 72 bottom: Damien Moorhouse

Chapter 10

82–83: Jani Estell; 84 top, 85: Ken Woisard; 84 middle and bottom, 86 top, 87: William Thuss; 86 bottom: Susan Merrill

Chapter 11

96–97: Jani Estell; 98, 99 bottom, 100: Susan Merrill; 99 top: Ana Flavia; 101 top left: Susan Herbert; bottom left: Jason Cheever; right: Chobi Capeta

Chapter 12

106, 107: Jani Estell; 108 top: "quil," bottom: Alice Campos Magalhaes; 109 top: Loretta Humble; bottom: Jen Siegrist

Chapter 13

114–115, 116 top: Susan Merrill; 116 bottom, 117, all: Jani Estell; 118: Richard Merrill; 119 top: William Thuss; remainder Susan Merrill

Appendix photos

p. 128–129: Susan Merrill. Troy Howard Middle School in Belfast, Maine, where students and staff built an EarthLoom as part of their Garden Project under the direction of teacher Steve Tanguay and Susan Barrett Merrill. Their Harvest Weaving blended cornstalks, flowers, hand-spun yarn and lots of cooperation into a gorgeous testament to the spirit of creativity and play inherent in all of us, of whatever age.

Rug and Kilim photos

Photos by Susan Merrill of rugs and kilims from the collection of Willam Mor: page 20, a Tibetan carpet; page 26–27, Uzbeki kilim, Uzbekistan.

Page 121: Richard Merrill.

Page 127 top, bottom: Richard Merrill.

Page 132 background: Richard Merrill. Inset: Frank Ferrel

RESOURCES

Available on the Weaving a Life
website: www.weavingalife.com

- Weaving a Life looms
- *The Art of Weaving a Life* book
- This book as a 2-CD audio book
- Kits for weaving the keyforms
- DVDs of Zati masks and EarthLooms
- Accessories and replacement parts
- Downloadable plans and instructions
  for building and weaving on the
  EarthLoom
- School loom sets
- Workshops at your location for each
  of the seven keyforms

Susan Barrett Merrill

Fiber sculptor and holistic life coach Susan Barrett Merrill attended Harvard, studied art at the Aegean School of Fine Arts in Greece, earned a bachelor of arts degree in education and art from Goddard College in Vermont, and received a master's from New Experimental College in Jutland, Denmark. Susan holds professional certifications in education and life coaching, is a member of the International Coach Federation, and has been designated a Maine Traditional Arts Master for her innovative approaches to weaving.

She is a pioneer in the field of fiber arts education for people with disabilities, and has represented the United States at symposia on arts and disabilities in Kobe, Japan, and Washington, DC. Susan's masks have seen performance and exhibition in the US and abroad, including at the Fiber Biennale in Chieri, Italy.

www.weavingalife.com | www.susanbarrettmerrill.com

Janet Lewis Estell

Jani contributed the keyform weaving instructions and instruction photographs for this book. The owner of Starcroft Fiber Mill in Columbia, Maine, she cards and spins for local farmers and produces her own line of yarn and knitting patterns. A life-long fiber artist, Jani was surrounded by a family of women who crafted. The gift of a spinning wheel from a friend led Jani to become a handspinner, felter, weaver, and fiber artist. She worked as a gardener at Stone Soup Farm and, with the encouragement and support of her mentor and friend Kate Nadeau, opened Starcroft. She has a degree in environmental sciences/forestry from Unity College. She is committed to running an earth-friendly green business.

E-mail Jani at jani@starcroftfiber.com.

Richard Merrill

Richard is a designer, artist, engineer, and puppeteer. He discovered a new richness in his teamwork with Susan on this project, and is excited to begin the next. He wrote the EarthLoom book, which is available on the Weaving a Life website. Merrill has designed aerospace cameras for high-tech firms and low-cost energy-efficient homes for the Maine climate. He and his bunraku-style puppet, Nasruddin, have performed widely, including at the national storytelling conference, Sharing the Fire. Richard is a founding partner of Intellergy, Inc., an energy technology R&D company in Blue Hill, Maine.

www.nasruddin.org | www.3hawk.com